UNCOVERING LOVE DISCOVERING SOUL

Mary and friends

LrP | LOVE revolution PRESS

ISBN: 978-0-9845815-0-4

Published by:
Love Revolution Press
P.O. Box 6790
Chico, CA 95927-6790
www.LoveRevolutionPress.com
info@LoveRevolutionPress.com

Cover design by Erin Mathis, www.emdesignstudio.com

Every vignette, encounter and detail in this book is true. Only the names of the people have been changed. We are all real human beings with real problems—for which our very real God is the total solution.

ACKNOWLEDGMENTS

Many people have played a part in the story behind this book. Some of you I have wounded. I am deeply sorry.

In the writing of this book, I especially want to acknowledge Daddy, Christopher, Andy and Kelly. Thank you for encouraging me to become who I really was in Christ all along. Thank you four for helping me to believe in God's love, purify my soul and step boldly into life and freedom.

As I see it now, life in God's love is as clear as a trail through a meadow on a bright spring morning when every chirping bird and blooming flower marks the way. But without your help through the struggles of life, I would not have found the trailhead.

PREFACE

I started writing *Uncovering Love, Discovering Soul* in April of 2008, the month after my marriage of 24 years officially came to an end. That same April, my oldest son, who "should have been" graduating from Harvard in May, began inpatient treatment at a mental hospital.

In the swirling tornadoes surrounding these events, I have done much God-asking and soul-searching. Violent storms had unsettled a "good Christian" way of living—one I thought I had pretty much figured out.

This book is about my journey from living an exemplary-looking Christian life to living deeply right and full of life. It is the story of my coming to an entirely new understanding of how God created us humans—to be brimming with His life and overflowing with His love.

It is not that I have completely embraced this way of being; it is just that now I am beginning to comprehend.

Since you have purified your souls in obeying the truth
through the Spirit in sincere love of the brethren,
love one another fervently with a pure heart.

1 Peter 1:22

CONTENTS

PART FOUR—THE FALL

PART FIVE—RESTORATION: GOD'S DONE DEAL

PART SIX—SOUL WARS: BELIEVING IN GOD'S DONE DEAL

PART SEVEN—LIVING THE SOLUTION

Part One

The Problem

Before any of this began, I was living my life like most of the Christians around me, and things seemed to be working pretty well. My husband and I were good, church-going people, and we had four nice, healthy children. The Bible said I should be joyful, and I was happy enough to convince myself I was. I didn't let myself admit I was overburdened because I knew I should "cast all my cares upon Him."

But then I realized I wasn't really loving. . . .

Something was deeply and dreadfully wrong.

CHAPTER 1

"Mary, You Don't Love."

Edna was 82 that summer of 2004; I was 44. But the age discrepancy didn't matter. Neither did our many and varied theological differences. For seven or eight years, Edna and I had been meeting almost every week for prayer, Bible study and just plain, honest talk. We were good for each other, and we knew it. We had become friends because Jesus was real to us. And because we were friends, we were honest with each other . . . sometimes brutally honest.

That August day was hot—so hot that the noisy air conditioner couldn't keep the living room of Edna's old mobile home cool. Dressed in her emerald-green, satin pajamas, Edna was sitting in her stuffed chair, rocking back and forth ever so slightly while sipping an iced tea. I was leaning back in my usual seat facing hers with an ice water in my hand.

I don't remember the talk or the Scriptures leading up to it, but I do remember Edna putting her drink down on the glass coffee table between us and leaning forward. Her perfectly combed, angel-white hair framed her intense blue eyes. "Mary, I want to tell you something."

She needed my assent to continue. "Okay," I said.

Even with the go-ahead from me, Edna hesitated a moment. Then slowly and deliberately, she spoke the words, "Mary, you don't love."

It was Edna's voice, but it was God addressing me.

"Mary, you don't love."

The raw truth of those words caught me off guard, but I did not argue against them. Stunned as I was by hearing them, somehow I just knew they were true. Fighting against them would be as futile as struggling to swim seaward with a tsunami rolling in.

I didn't love.

Verses from 1 Corinthians 13 flashed through my mind:

Though I speak with the tongues of men and of angels, but have not love, I have become sounding brass or a clanging cymbal. And though I have the gift of prophecy, and understand all mysteries and all knowledge, and though I have all faith, so that I could remove mountains, but have not love, I am nothing. And though I bestow all my goods to feed the poor, and though I give my body to be burned, but have not love, it profits me nothing (1 Corinthians 13:1-3).

All this washed over me in seconds—much faster than it takes to read the words. Even though I was a devout follower of Jesus, I was not loving in the way God intended.

I thought of all my nice deeds. I tried my hardest to be diligent, kind and responsible. I stayed up late to help the kids with their homework and got up early to fix breakfast and make lunches. We went to church faithfully. I visited sick friends, wrote letters of encouragement to those in prison and gave money to homeless people I passed on the street. And I worked as a writer/editor for a mission organization.

But in that moment in Edna's living room, I somehow understood that in doing all these things, I was nothing but a clanging cymbal—a horribly loud, irritating noisemaker.

I slid out of the stuffed rocking chair and lay facedown on the yellow shag carpet. What else could I do? I'd gotten the most important thing in life wrong all these years. In fact, I'd gotten it so wrong that I didn't even know what right was.

So there on the floor, with Edna in her emerald pajamas lending assent and passing me kleenex, I prayed, "God, whatever it takes, I want to love You and I want to love people. I don't know what's wrong, but I trust You to fix it. Whatever it takes, work out Your love in me."

Let me make something clear. It wasn't that I lacked knowledge *about* love. That day at Edna's, I knew quite a bit of what the Bible had to say *about* love. And I was honestly trying to live lovingly to the best of my ability.

I knew that God loved me unconditionally and always. *Jesus loves me this I know, for the Bible tells me so.* I had sung the song in Sunday school as a child. I understood that God created humans to be loved by Him—to fellowship with Him and to walk with Him just as He walked with Adam and Eve in the cool of the garden.

I also knew that it was very important to love God. When a scribe came to Jesus asking which commandment was most important, He responded, *And you shall love the LORD your God with* ***all your heart,*** *with* ***all your soul,*** *with* ***all your mind,*** *and with* ***all your strength.*** *This is the first commandment* (Mark 12:30).

No, head knowledge about God's love for us humans and the importance of loving God with all that was in us was not my problem. And understanding my responsibility to love others was not a problem either. That also had been ingrained in me from my youth.

Again referring to the Old Covenant, Jesus said, *And the second, like it, is this: You shall love your neighbor as yourself* (Mark 12:31).

So I knew that God loved me, and I tried to obey these two most important commandments just as I attempted to do most things in my Christian life. In the way I saw these verses, they referred to *my* fortitude and character. And so I tried to love God with *all my* heart, *all my* soul, *all my* mind and *all my* strength. I worked hard to love my neighbor like I loved myself too—by being nice, caring and dependable and by putting the needs of others above my own.

And when things didn't work right, I prayed to God for strength to redouble my efforts and do more good deeds. I kept pushing myself and struggling to be obedient, thus proving to God that I loved Him. I kept trying to be good and show love to others like I knew I was supposed to.

I thought this was how God's love worked. The Bible said, *If you keep My commandments, you will abide in My love* (John 15:10). So I tried to do right and keep the Ten Commandments, assuming that by so doing, I would be abiding in His love.

I figured this outward obedience demonstrated that I loved God and my neighbor. I assumed that the good deeds I was able to generate were love. I took for granted that they were what God had planned for me to do. I just presumed I was living life the way God intended—like Christians were supposed to.

And from what I could tell, most people who sat around me in church on Sunday thought like I did. We believed God loved us, we did what was right (or tried our best to) and so we presumed we loved Him, and others too, like He intended.

But that day at Edna's, I realized I had been fooling myself. I was failing miserably at loving. I didn't have understanding of what the error was. I just knew that something was keeping me from loving. I wasn't living in line with His most important teaching. God's highest desire for me as His born-again child was being thwarted.

I also knew that somehow God had to be the solution to this problem. God is a Perfect Creator. He knows what He is doing, and He does not make mistakes. God made me for a purpose which I was intended to live out.

When our Perfect Creator makes something—the fish, the birds or the cattle on a thousand hills—He always designs the creature so that it can fulfill the purpose for which it was made.

God gave fish gills. Why? To live in the sea. God gave birds wings. Why? To navigate the skies. So whatever it took for me to live out my purpose had to be inherent in my design too.

God perfectly made us humans to have a love relationship with Himself and to share that love with others. Therefore, this created purpose has to be in our nature—woven into our very being—at the core of humanity's original formation. Love has to be something that flows naturally as part of how He designed us to live.

So why wasn't that love coming out of me? Why wasn't I functioning as intended? Here I was, created to love, but not living that out. Like a fish out of water or a bird with clipped wings, I wasn't living as God had planned.

I could no longer deny it. I had been lulled to sleep through the years by my solid church upbringing and had come to accept the life I was living as the one God intended for me. But Edna's words, "Mary, you don't love," had shaken me out of my coma-like slumber. They had awakened in me a long-quieted desire and sparked a host of questions:

What was the cause of my lack of love? How had I gotten into my current condition? And, above all, how was God to be the cure?

I didn't have a clue as to what the answers might be that day when I left Edna's yellow mobile home shimmering in the summer heat. I didn't have a clue because I didn't really know how much God loved me (although I thought I did). I also couldn't even begin to comprehend the answer because I didn't understand how God had created me—especially the part of me I now know to be my soul.

But I was confident God would somehow get me to loving; love was in the center of His will for me. And I had prayed, "Whatever it takes."

I knew God would lead me. . . .

I just didn't know the rugged path ahead.

CHAPTER 2

India, Six Months Later

In India six months later, the shiny façade of my "good Christian" life cracked wide open.

A group of us from the mission organization I work with had flown into the Mumbai airport early that morning from Hyderabad. It would be a few hours before we caught the next plane down to Kerala.

For a week we had been traveling around India, but I hadn't called home. For some reason my cell phone, which was supposed to work overseas, was non-functional. Now was a good time to call; about 9:30 Monday morning in Mumbai made it about 8:00 Sunday evening in California.

"Perfect," I thought. "My family will be home—Dennis and the kids too. I'll get to talk to Bryn, Anne and Mark and find out how Jake's doing away at college."

Leaving my luggage with the rest of the group, I made my way through throngs of brown- skinned people over to an area labeled in several languages; the one I recognized read "telephones." I waited in line and then gave the turbaned, older gentleman behind the table two 500-rupee bills and my home phone number. He dialed and passed me the receiver.

Brrrring. Brrrring. Brrrring. From half a world away, I heard the familiar jingle.

Bryn, our 17-year-old daughter, answered, "Mom."

I could tell immediately that something was wrong. I pressed the receiver tight against my ear to shut out the sounds of the crowded airport.

"Oh, Mom, Jake's in the hospital."

She was crying. It was hard to hear.

"He wasn't eating. He hadn't come out of his room. They took him to the ER. Dad's back there now . . . in Boston at the hospital."

I wanted to say something. I wanted to cry. I wanted to scream. But instead a weight, a heaviness, a sadness sunk down upon me, and nothing came out.

Jake was our oldest, a tall, dark, handsome youth of 19—a freshman at Harvard and on the crew team. He was, in my eyes and in the eyes of our church and community, about as close as one could come to being the "perfect" young man. But inside, he was deeply troubled.

My husband, Dennis, and I had put band aids over our son's issues so very few people knew about them. They weren't something we talked about. It was almost as if we thought that if we didn't mention the problems, they would go away or, even better, never have existed in the first place.

We had tried to aid Jake in the ways we thought best. By helping him stay busy with so many good things—rigorous academics, church activities, singing and rowing crew at national levels—we figured he wouldn't have time to let depression and social issues surface. But now they had burst through that cover-up with great force.

I thought also of my husband back in Boston now with our son. He was a standout too, a nationally known physician. We had met as freshmen at Stanford in 1978 and married five years later.

I'd supported him through medical school and two residencies, and at the same time, he had helped me through graduate school, a post-doc and later through the trials of multiple sclerosis (MS). We had four beautiful children—two boys and two girls. Our big country farmhouse sitting on 20 acres boasted a redwood wraparound porch and tree-shaded decks. The kids were involved in church youth groups. We had Bible studies in our home and tithed—even more than 10 percent.

But a few days before leaving for India, I had found out there was another woman. Dennis had assured me it was over . . . that he would never see her again . . . that I shouldn't cancel the trip.

So here I was, in the Mumbai airport, with my "good Christian" family crumbling to bits.

I tried to pull my thoughts together. They needed me at home. Bryn couldn't take care of Anne (a sophomore in high school) and Mark (a seventh grader), drive them to school and still maintain her rigorous senior-year schedule. And I needed to be in Boston with my son and husband too.

"Bryn, honey, I'm coming back to the States."

"No, Mom, don't. Dad said to tell you that we'll see you next week."

We talked a bit more. My 1,000-rupee time was up.

"Hang in there. I love you. Tell Dad, Jake, Anne and Mark I love them too. Bye, honey."

I passed the phone back to the turbaned gentleman and walked in stunned silence through the throngs of people until I found a seat in a boarding area far away from the rest of my group. I sat down, put my face in my hands, hunched over to shut out the airport hustle as best I could and prayed.

"Lord, please make it okay. Help Jake get well. Help Dennis be strong. Be with the kids at home. Jesus, please get us through this." With everything in the conscious part of me I pleaded, "Jesus, make things right again. Get us back to where we were before."

But from the core of my being came another cry—a louder, more primeval prayer. Honest, raw and untamed, it shouted to be heard above the clamor of my "proper" plea to "make things right again."

"Why?" it screamed. "What is going on? Life shouldn't be this way."

"Isn't God's love supposed to conquer all this?" the cry continued. "Then why doesn't it? Why is life a ceaseless struggle to do right? I can't even do the right. And even when I pull myself together and manage somehow to eke out a bit of good, it isn't enough anyway."

"I don't want affairs," my heart shouted. "I don't want depression. I don't want hurt inside of people. And God, You don't either. So why? Why? WHY? I don't understand!"

I thought back then to the affair I'd had myself years earlier. I had blown one of the Ten Commandments—according to my upbringing, one of the most important. Why had I done that anyway? Was this why my marriage was struggling and my family was in turmoil? Why couldn't I be good? Why couldn't I love like the Bible told me to? What was wrong with me? Maybe what was happening now was some sort of punishment for being intrinsically and irreparably evil at the core.

Everything was a crazy jumble in my mind, like the confusion of the bustling airport with unfamiliar, dark-haired, brown-eyed people—people,

people everywhere wearing strange clothes and speaking languages I could not understand.

It all seemed so hopeless. Life was a confused mess of warring, internal struggles. I had tried hard for 44 years to be good. But my life was falling apart. In my innermost being, I knew God had definitely not created me to live this way. "Born again" and "Spirit filled" as I was, life wasn't working. Somehow I knew these problems were just further symptoms of the same disease I had become aware of six months earlier in Edna's living room.

I needed God in a new and bigger way. The issues plaguing my family and my lack of love could not be solved by the means I had employed in the past. These problems were too far-reaching and foundational for that approach.

Yet still I was tempted to return to the old, familiar method and ask God for His strength to press on and work harder. My natural inclination was to keep trying to be more responsible, kind and caring.

After all, that is how I had been raised to tackle life.

CHAPTER 3

My "Good Christian" Self

I grew up in a solid, all-American home filled with Christian values. This set the framework for how I viewed God and life in general.

Mama was a beautiful, high-class woman who had graduated summa cum laude from Stanford University in an era when most women didn't go to college. She had been an Episcopalian until she'd met Daddy, a Berkeley student and Italian-Catholic-turned-on-fire Baptist.

She'd given her life to Jesus. They'd gotten married. I was born nine months later in 1960. My sister, Kelly, came along 13 months after me and my brother, Peter, 15 months after her. We were all born in Loma Linda, California, where Daddy was in dental school. Later he became a faculty member at the university. We weren't Adventists, like almost everyone else associated with Loma Linda University, but I didn't mind eating veggie burgers and going to church on Saturday with my parents and their friends.

We would worship on Sundays too, at whatever church seemed right to my parents at the time. I remember attending Sunday school at Zion Reformed, Nazarene, Presbyterian and Baptist churches.

In all of this, however, it never felt to me like Daddy and Mama were looking for a denomination that fit their style or comfort zone. Rather, it felt like we, me included, were searching for God the way He really was—bigger than all the Christ-centered churches yet represented in each by a unique group of people.

As a child, my most memorable contacts with God actually came outside of church. When I was about 7 years old, I remember going to a Kathryn Kuhlman meeting at a giant cement-and-marble building in Los Angeles. Daddy, Mama, Kelly, Peter and I had waited a long time in line and then sat in the front row of the balcony. I'd leaned forward, rested my chin on the top of the balcony railing and watched. Ms. Kuhlman, dressed in a long, flowing white gown, seemed like an angel-princess to me. I wanted to look like that and be like her. I wanted to stay in the presence of God that I felt in the auditorium.

Etched into my memory was a little blind boy—a few years younger than me—who was healed that night. He hadn't been able to see before, but way down on the big, wooden platform, the boy's mother held up three fingers from across the stage, and he counted clearly into the microphone, "One, two, three."

When I was in fifth grade, Daddy and Mama decided to leave the smog of Southern California, and we moved to an apple ranch in San Luis Obispo. Daddy opened an orthodontic practice in town where we went to school. Weekends we spent as a family—planting, pruning, watering, picking or selling apples.

Despite having gone to church all of my life and believing in God, I didn't accept Jesus into my heart until I was 16.

After receiving Christ, I especially liked escaping to the hills behind the apple orchard with my Great Dane, Degan; my quarter horse, Sunshine;

and my Bible. Things felt right all alone with the hills cutting off my view of the world. I would close my eyes and sing, riding bareback across a grassy slope. Or I'd stop under a spreading oak and let Sunshine graze while I rested my head on Degan's side and read. Sometimes when I knew I was far enough away from home that nobody would hear me, I'd shout, "Jesus, I love You," into the fresh, sage-tinged air. Then I'd cry because I felt so close to God, and the tears would splatter onto my bare legs and mix with the wet of horse sweat. On those rides, everything was natural and free like I wanted it to be.

Down in the valley, however, I felt pulled to do things I knew weren't right—like copy someone's calculus homework or get physical on a date. Thoughts of doing these things scared me; I didn't want to mess up. So I tried to keep these urges under control through discipline. I punished my body and whipped it into shape.

And I had what I thought were biblical grounds for this approach. One of my favorite verses from those high school days was Paul's exhortation from 1 Corinthians 9:27: *I beat my body and make it my slave so that after I have preached to others, I myself will not be disqualified for the prize* (NIV). So I felt thoroughly justified in "beating my body" and making it conform to family values and church standards in the way I believed that verse implied.

Kelly, Peter and I played a lot of tennis in high school. But regular practice wasn't enough for me. I would run three miles down the canyon from our house to the tennis club, play a couple hours of tennis and run back up the canyon. Then I would drag myself into the house and collapse on the couch, feeling miserable but great at the same time—miserable because I was tired, sweaty and hungry, but great because I had made my body do it.

Working in the orchard I would do the same thing. I'd drive the tractor, mowing weeds between the apple rows, oblivious to the dust that rose up covering my body and the branches that slapped me across the face. During apple season, we'd often rise at first light and work until it got too hot for the apples to store well—usually around noon or so—without breakfast or even a drink of water. To me these were the right things to do; I felt good about "crucifying" my flesh in this way.

The teaching I heard in church confirmed that God wanted me to be a disciplined, hardworking, nice person. So I threw myself into doing commendable deeds and avoiding evil ones. Only a few years after having come to faith in Jesus, I was a teacher for kindergarten Sunday school, a camp counselor for younger high school students and president of the church's youth group.

In college, the doing good and body beating turned more into disciplining myself to achieve the goal I had set; in this case, the prize was good grades. I wasn't particularly smart compared to most of my Stanford colleagues, but I could make myself study. I spent hours and hours secluded away at my favorite study haunt—an old wooden desk among the musty volumes on the top floor of Cubberly Library. This all paid off in terms of GPA and academic awards—the things I judged valuable at the time. My friends, however, balanced their time with an array of activities such as football games, fraternity parties, guest lectures or old movies at the Sunday night "flicks."

Originally, I had gone off to college wanting to be a medical doctor and help children's hurting bodies. But after working for a pediatrician one summer, I realized I was more interested in the inner framework of the child. How children thought, reacted to things, played and related to others intrigued me. So I chose to attend graduate school in developmental psychology at the University of Washington.

After the first year of graduate school, I married Dennis. It seemed the beginnings of a perfect life dedicated to serving God by helping hurting children. We had met when we were 18, as freshmen at Stanford. Now he was in medical school. We dreamed and strategized about going overseas as missionaries and setting up orphanages and health clinics.

Four years later, along with our two young children (Jake and Bryn), we left Seattle for Los Angeles. Dennis began residency at UCLA, and I started a post-doc at its Neuropsychiatric Institute. Each day I worked with children plagued by malfunctions of the brain such as autism, fetal-alcohol syndrome and epilepsy.

One event in particular stands out in my mind from that time. I was evaluating a set of identical twin girls, just under 2 years of age—with Down's syndrome. Their father, a young Hispanic man, had brought the children in for testing because his wife was too depressed to accompany them.

When I shared the results of the cognitive tests, he started crying. I'll never forget the silent tears running down his face and wetting the silver cross with the figure of Jesus upon it that hung around his neck. The reality of the long-term impact of this condition for his two precious daughters was heartbreaking. I started crying too and had to excuse myself to go to the bathroom where I gained enough composure to come back and finish the conference.

Needless to say, this was not an appropriate professional reaction. Soon after this incident, I chose to stop seeing disabled children and began instead to work on a series of studies of malnourished toddlers in Kenya. By funneling all my energies into studying starving children living on a continent half a world away, I could avoid the real-life contact that hurt so much. Thus I believed I could keep myself emotionally safe while still caring for others.

In the four years I devoted to analyzing data, designing studies and writing papers on these poor, starving children, I never looked into the gaunt eyes of a young Kenyan mother nor held a malnourished baby on my lap. In fact, rationalizing that I couldn't leave my own children—especially our youngest additions, Anne and Mark—I turned down every request to visit Kenya. In this way, I felt I could help without having to really engage with people and cry along with them.

During this time in my life, I looked at myself from the outside and was proud of what I saw—four beautiful children, advancing careers, uplifting friends and a good church. I didn't see any problems because there weren't any visible on the surface. I was trying hard to make it happen like I thought God wanted, and things seemed to be working.

But in actuality, the shiny, clean outward appearance was a big part of the problem; it made me think I was shiny and clean within as well. The outside looked so right that I saw no need of looking beyond it into the depth of myself . . . and into the depth of God.

But the cracking of that strong, well-polished cover-up would begin to expose the real mess underneath.

CHAPTER 4

MS and Other Disasters

Looking back now, given the way I had driven myself to produce commendable deeds, it wasn't surprising that I got multiple sclerosis, a stress-related, autoimmune disease, in 1992. I was diagnosed with MS a few months after Mark, our youngest child, was born. I had just turned 32.

My husband was finishing his second residency, and we were preparing to move. Both of us had academic positions waiting for us at UC Davis. Dennis would be working at the Medical Center, and I would be doing research in the Department of Human Development on the main campus.

But for me, the job was not to be. I had worn myself out trying to do good things. Having four babies in seven years and going to school or working full-time during most of that period had taken its toll; I was shot.

For months after the diagnosis and our move to the Sacramento area, I lay on the couch trying to "take it easy" while the children played around me. The doctors had told me to rest, and so I attempted to do that, much as I'd tried before to be a good kid, a good student or a good mother.

But nothing helped—not rest, not the drugs the physicians prescribed, not diet, not vitamins. The MS only got worse. My eyes crossed. I couldn't walk in a straight line. I stuttered. A horrible burning pain on the right side of my face came and went throughout the day and night. My body wouldn't work.

My sister and her husband, along with their young family, moved from Saint Louis, Missouri, to help take care of us. Dennis and I had purchased a place in the country before I knew I had MS. The property came with two houses, so we lived in one and they moved into the other. I couldn't take care of the kids, and Dennis was busy settling into his new, demanding job. Kelly and her family have never made a show of this sacrifice, but it was a great one on their part.

Sadness, confusion and hopelessness threatened to overwhelm me. At night I lay awake in bed and tried to muffle my crying from Dennis. During the day, I rested on the couch and wore dark glasses to hide my tears from the kids.

So much of what I had planned and worked toward was being stripped away. I, who had been such a doer-of-good, suddenly couldn't do much of anything. We hired a babysitter. Kelly helped drive the kids to school. She also fixed us dinner almost every night. The kids would walk down the potholed country road to Auntie Kelly's house and bring our dinner back in a little red wagon.

Through all this, I became desperate for God. Initially I wanted Him on my terms—for healing so I could get back to normal and live my life as I had before. But as the longing increased, I more and more just wanted God for who He really was. Intense desire to know Him in a fuller way shouted out.

As part of the MS, I would be awakened two or three times a night with burning trigeminal neuralgia pain. It felt like a hot iron being pressed against my right cheek. The burning would last for 45 minutes at a stretch and then completely resolve until the next attack several hours later. During these times, I could do nothing but pray. And so each night—alone in the dark and pain—I spent time with God.

But the longing didn't lessen; it grew. I couldn't explain the thirst. I had God, but I desperately wanted Him in a deep, deep way!

Then one evening a guest speaker visited our church. After the message, I felt like I should go to the altar. I had never gone to the front in a service before that I could remember. Even going forward was a big step.

"What do you want?" the guest preacher asked me.

"I just want God," I sobbed.

"Lift up your hands and say, 'I surrender all,' " he told me.

I didn't want to do it. A horrible resistance rose within me. Why did I have to surrender? Hadn't almost everything been stripped from me anyway? Why did I have to raise my hands? God could give me more of Himself at home if He wanted, in the quiet of the night. That's how I had accepted Christ—away from onlookers and devoid of hype in the peace and calm of my familiar bedroom.

But I did it; I raised my hands and said, "I surrender all."

At that moment, from the center of the cross hanging behind the altar—from right where the vertical and horizontal beams met—God's love poured down on me. It came like little drops of liquid light and rested in my heart. I couldn't talk. I couldn't move. Pure love cascaded down, vast like an ocean, but gentle as the dew. It fell in wave after wave of undulating light—love, love, love. Intense. Powerful. Gentle. Pure. Freeing.

It kept coming. I can't explain it. Being loved like that defies words. Several hours later, I got up off the floor. The child caregivers had gone home, and Jake, Bryn, Anne and Mark were entertaining themselves in the back of the sanctuary. The pastor was waiting to lock the doors.

After that experience, the effects of the MS lessened, and I became increasingly awakened to God's personal love for me. I had said, "I just want God," and He'd given me love—not judgment, not wisdom, not direction about something to do—only love.

He loved me just as much as I lay on the couch doing absolutely nothing as He had when I'd been taking care of the family, writing articles and helping hurting children. He loved me, not for what I did or didn't do, but for who I was.

In fact, I started to realize God had not made me a human *doing;* He had made me a human *being*. He loved me simply because I was His child.

I learned this, but unfortunately, somehow I didn't learn it deeply enough. Somehow I didn't allow the love of God to change the core of my being so that I really believed it. I'd had the experience and I could quote the Scriptures, but their deep meaning hadn't become part of me. Still, in some distorted way, even in my weakened state, I kept trying to earn love by being good.

But I couldn't always be good.

I was 38 when Mama died. That was the year I had the affair.

I had met him in church a few months before she died. I needed a shoulder to cry on. He was a divorced man with two children. Three months after Mama's death, it was over.

I felt horrible. How could I have done such evil? I had disobeyed what I considered one of God's most important commandments. I told Dennis. He forgave me, but I couldn't forgive myself. I felt like a hypocrite going to church. How could God ever be pleased with a sinner like me? I had pushed His grace too far. He couldn't possibly love me now. It was a tough year.

But I clung to my forgiving Father and with renewed strength and determination pushed back in the only way I knew how—by doing even more commendable deeds. I worked harder than ever to regain what I'd lost by patching over the cracks in the armor of my Christian life so that nothing improper escaped.

The sins and weights I carried and tried to keep contained should have been a clue that problems within called for attention, but I didn't take the hint. Instead, I welded the pieces of the cover-up back together, repolished the armor and plunged on in life.

I threw myself into being what I thought a Christian wife and mother should be. People, especially those at church, commended my husband and me for our beautiful family and the example we were to the community. Dennis and I team-taught adult Sunday school. With our joint M.D./Ph.D. credentials, parent groups sometimes asked us to speak about raising successful children in our highly academic community.

Jake, Bryn, Anne and Mark were good kids—polite, kind and full of healthy energy and curiosity. I liked their friends. Each of them qualified for accelerated programs at school. In addition, they all excelled in athletics.

The kids were also actively involved in church youth groups and Bible studies. We were attending the church known to have the best youth group around, and often we would host special events at our house. Thirty or 40 kids would square-dance in the barn or sit out on the big green lawn singing worship songs and watching the stars come out.

Dennis got up early each morning and headed off to the hospital to better the lives of hurting patients. He would usually return home by 7:00 p.m. if he wasn't away lecturing or attending a conference.

About the time Jake entered high school, as the kids became increasingly involved with school and extracurricular activities, I began working part-time for a mission organization. From the comfort of our large country home with the wraparound porch and the sheep grazing peacefully in the neighboring green pasture, I would write articles and grants or edit books.

I liked the work; it made me feel useful. The family seemed to be doing well. The MS wasn't bothering me as much. In short, I again liked what I saw of my family and myself. On the surface, life was hectic and busy but generally the way I thought it should be. It seemed that all the hard work of being a Christian and trying to be good was paying off.

But, if I had stopped long enough to consider, I would have realized that a lot was wrong. Beneath the polished cover, I carried great mounds of internal stress. Trying to make everything right—help the kids succeed in school, write well and meet deadlines, care for the big house and yard, and attend church, pray and worship as Scripture seemed to say I needed to do—was a lot of work. Really, the work was never done. And beneath conscious awareness, fear was constant—a silent dread of failing to measure up, of sinning and of somehow not being worthy of God's love.

Yet I was oblivious to these internal problems. To me, this was life the way I had always known it. The Bible told me to be full of peace and joy, so I wouldn't let myself admit that I wasn't experiencing that. I honestly thought I was living the "life more abundant" promised in Scripture.

I hadn't the foggiest notion that life might be fundamentally different than I was living it. I couldn't recall any Christian books or preaching that indicated otherwise. I just lived, thought and interpreted Scripture like those around me seemed to.

But that day in Edna's living room, I saw the truth; I didn't love. And in the Mumbai airport, I realized my family was in shambles. I had no idea what the cure for these problems might be. The way of healing for the disease wasn't even on my radar screen. I only knew that I and my family were desperately sick and that turning back to the old way was not an option.

God had to do something completely outside the box of my understanding.

Part Two

Transitions

Clearly God hadn't designed me for the shiny façade of existence I was calling "life." But what *did* the life He intended look like, and how was I to step into that?

I didn't have a clue. Yet I was confident that buried deep, like hidden treasure, God held the answer as to why I was not loving and to the dysfunctions in my family.

I had to know Him as the cure. There was no other hope.

The trials in my life spurred me on. . . .

CHAPTER 5

"Come On, Jesus!"

After that day at Edna's, underscored by the problems highlighted in the Mumbai airport, I knew I needed daily prayer. Several people from a little church in town gathered each morning, seven days a week, at 6:30 and prayed until around 9:00. I couldn't get there until about 8:00, but being late didn't matter. People came and went as their work or school schedules allowed.

I had first met Pastor Andy and a few others in the prayer meetings. They were often seated on the old chairs or on the floor of the church office when I arrived after dropping off Mark at school. Most were definitely not like the Christians I'd mingled with before. Some were not particularly well-educated or well-dressed. Many were not much older than my own kids. And the variety of cultures and races made white, Anglo-Saxon me no longer part of the majority.

Diverse as we were, we had two things in common: We loved Jesus, and we were open about our struggles.

Together we prayed for our families and ourselves. We prayed for Jake as his depression waxed and waned. We agonized together as psychologists and psychiatrists saw him and as he tried various medications, none of which seemed to work. We asked God for help as he dropped out of Harvard and returned home, then later went back only to drop out again. We prayed as issues with drug and alcohol abuse surfaced.

We prayed for Dennis too. More evidence of the affair came to light. He said he was sorry and was going to stop seeing her. Dennis and I prayed together as a couple. We argued. We made up. She surfaced again.

In the meetings, after prayer, we talked. One day I told them about the affair I'd had years earlier. I cried when I told them and felt horrible all over again, but everybody hugged me and thanked me for being honest. They didn't shake their fingers at me and tell me how I shouldn't have done it. (I already knew that.)

In fact, the way they treated me filled me with hope that a solution existed—not just forgiveness and a band aid for strength to go on in the same old way, but for a real cure. Within me confidence grew; God would take care of what was wrong if I let Him deal with the root cause.

And so we prayed, asking God to humble us and get the "yuck" out of us. We didn't know exactly what we were praying for or how it was going to happen, but we asked Him to clean us out and make us right so we could love. Thus we prayed, morning after morning, for the center of His will in us—that we would love Him and others. "Come on, Jesus!" I kept praying. "Come on, Jesus!"

And God's love began to jump off the pages of the Bible at me. I saw that He wants us to know a four-dimensional love that goes beyond knowledge. Paul prays, *That you, being rooted and grounded in love, may be able to comprehend with all the saints what is the* ***width*** *and* ***length*** *and* ***depth*** *and* ***height****—to know the love of Christ which passes knowledge; that you may be filled with all the fullness of God* (Ephesians 3:17-19). I could only visualize in three dimensions, but God wants us to comprehend His four-dimensional love that surpasses knowledge.

I also saw that nothing—absolutely nothing—separates us from His love. Romans 8:38-39 says, *For I am persuaded that neither death nor life, nor angels nor principalities nor powers, nor things present nor things to come, nor height nor depth, nor any other created thing, shall be able to separate us from the love of God which is in Christ Jesus our Lord.*

God's love is everywhere; it surrounds us like air. And I realized that believing in love is like breathing. Just as a baby comes alive with its first breath and then continues to live by breathing, we too, as believers, come alive with our initial belief in Jesus and then remain alive by continuing to trust in more of His love for us. Air is present whether or not we choose to breathe, just as love is present whether or not we choose to believe.

God's love is amazing!

But despite these insights, desperation grew within me. I wanted God with an intense desire like I had craved Him after being diagnosed with MS. I wanted Him in a whole new way I couldn't explain. Somehow I knew ethereal, heavenly love, but I didn't know it in graspable, applicable reality. I knew God's love as it had poured down on me from the center of the cross in that memorable occasion at church, but I didn't know it in a usable, tangible, day-to-day form that worked in my world.

During the years that I wrestled with my lack of love and struggled with the ongoing issues in my life, I prayed alone too. We lived out in the country west of town, and evening after evening as I walked with no one but the crows and jackrabbits watching, desires welled up in my heart.

Sunset after sunset, I longed for Jesus to come and touch me with His love in a way that was different than before. I didn't care if He came as a lightning bolt with signs and wonders or as a cool breeze on a hot summer evening with calm and peace. I just wanted Him to do something—something I knew He was capable of doing but hadn't done yet. I desired for Him to meet me with His love—not as He'd done on the floor of the church, but in a whole new way I had never experienced.

In India, Bible college students had greeted us by throwing flower petals on the paths before us. So I often plucked rose petals from the bushes in the front yard and tossed them out to welcome Jesus as I walked. Some evenings I would turn down a dirt side road into an alfalfa field. There I would kneel or lie facedown in the green alfalfa aching and longing for Jesus' love in a way I had never known it before. Over and over again I kept praying, "Come on, Jesus." I wanted "the rubber to meet the road." I wasn't sure what those words meant, but that was my desire.

When I traveled to India again in February of 2007, I went with a cry on my heart to know of the love I did not know—in tangible, living expression.

On that trip, we left from Chicago and flew nonstop to Delhi. The 17-hour flight took us halfway around the world. For most of the trip, when I wasn't sleeping, I listened over and over again to one particular song on my battery-operated CD player. Just before leaving, a Josh Groban song titled *My Confession* had grabbed me:

I have been blind, unwilling,
To see the true love you're giving.
I have ignored every blessing.
I'm on my knees confessing
That I feel myself surrender
Each time I see your face.
I am staggered by your beauty, your unassuming grace.
And I feel my heart is turning, falling into place.
I can't hide. Now hear my confession.

As our Boeing 777 flew over the United States, crossed the Atlantic and navigated the skies above the Arctic, Europe and into Asia, I listened to those words and offered them to God. Again and again, 37,000 feet above the earth, I sang that song of confession.

On the way back to the States two weeks later, I did the same—over and over confessing for myself . . . and for others. *I have been blind, unwilling, to see the true love you're giving. . . . And I feel my heart is turning, falling into place. I can't hide. Now hear my confession.* I didn't know why I was doing it. It just seemed right—agonizingly right. From the bottom of my heart, Edna's words still rang with painful clarity, "Mary, you don't love."

A few months after returning from that trip, I attended the annual conference at our church. Gaylord Enns was one of the speakers at that three-day event. He was an older gentleman with a graying beard, and his soft-spoken words carried powerful truth I had never heard before.

I remember Gaylord standing at the podium in a loose-fitting Hawaiian shirt and addressing us in an unhurried voice. He said something like the following: "In the first part of His ministry, Jesus speaks of two commandments. An expert in the Law comes to Him with a question: 'Which of the commandments in the Law is most important?' "

"And in answer to that question Jesus responded . . ." Gaylord paused, flipped the pages of his Bible and read: *"And you shall love the LORD your God with all your heart, with all your soul, with all your mind, and with all your strength. This is the first commandment. And the second, like it, is this: You shall love your neighbor as yourself"* (Mark 12:30-31).

I knew those Scriptures very well, and I had tried to live them out—especially in the past two years. But what Gaylord said next, I'd never considered before.

"These *two* commandments are the greatest in the Old Testament," Gaylord continued. "They sum up all the others in the **Old Covenant** Law of Moses. But later, on the night of the last supper—the night before His death—Jesus introduces the **New Covenant.**" Gaylord took off his glasses to look us straight on.

"As part of that **New Covenant,** He gives only *one* command—which He owns as His **New Commandment.**" Again Gaylord thumbed through the pages and read: *"A* ***new commandment*** *I give to you, that you love one another; as I have loved you, that you also love one another"* (John 13:34).

"How can this be?" Gaylord asked. "Is Jesus contradicting Himself?" He paused for a moment to let the impact of this seeming inconsistency in Scripture settle into us. "How is it that *two* commandments have become *one* and that *one* does not include loving God?"

Gaylord paused again—long enough for me to realize, with vivid clarity, that I had no clue about the answer.

Then he continued, slowly and unhurriedly, "Because in loving one another, we are loving God the way He wants to be loved. When I love my brother and sister in Christ, I am loving the Christ in them."

Wow! That truth came over me like a rainbow of peace after a raging storm. And there was more. . . .

"In addition," Gaylord went on, "this New Commandment was strikingly different from the Old. It was written on the hearts of men. God established the New Covenant from the inside of us. By God's indwelling, the New Covenant supplies the *source* of the love. God Himself provides the love necessary for us to actually love others."

Wow! Wow! I sat back in my chair completely amazed by the power and simplicity of loving God's way. We love others with the love He shares with us. My hard work wasn't necessary to generate the love. It wasn't about me loving with *all my* heart, *all my* mind, *all my* soul and *all my* strength. It didn't depend on me trying to put my neighbor's needs before my own. *I* wasn't the focus at all.

God would supply.

Later when it came out, I read Gaylord's book, *Love Revolution: Rediscovering the Lost Command of Jesus*. Apart from the Bible, this is the most impactful book I have ever read. My heart was primed for the truth of it.

God Himself is the source of the love! All I have to do is let His love come into me and then share it with others by letting it flow out. This is how God designed loving to be under the New Covenant—here and now on earth. This is how He intends for "the rubber to meet the road."

But my life wasn't working like that.

Something messed up deep inside of me was hindering His love for the world that was supposed to express itself in tangible ways through me.

CHAPTER 6

Old Word, New Understanding

After hearing Gaylord speak and reading *Love Revolution* several times, I knew unequivocally that under the New Covenant God's love in us was to be the source for our loving others.

I had accepted Christ. His love was in me. *God is love* (1 John 4:16), and everything of Him was available to me.

All I had to do was open the floodgates and let that love out.

Easy, right?

Wrong!

Some unknown obstacle deep within was preventing me from really loving as God had created me to. What was blocking God's heavenly, infinite love from flowing through me and triumphing on earth?

Somehow I was beginning to suspect the problem was in my soul. In fact, the word "soul" had begun to hold a prominent place in my thinking.

One day about nine months after hearing Gaylord speak at the conference, I sat down at the kitchen table to look up a handful of verses with the word "soul" in them.

But my planned, short Bible study turned into an ongoing quest. Since that afternoon, I have written out and prayed over thousands of Scriptures—not only Scriptures with the word "soul" in them, but also verses with words such as "spirit," "body," "heart," "will," "mind" and "flesh" as well. Some days I spent hours at the kitchen table with a concordance, Bible encyclopedias and Greek and Hebrew word study guides spread out before me.

I wanted to know the mystery of how God intended us humans to function. How had He originally designed us to live out the one New Commandment: Love one another as I have loved you? I sensed that it had something to do with my soul, yet the soul was the part I wasn't understanding. What was the soul anyway?

These questions played in my mind one evening as I sat in the rented hall that was our church building waiting for the Sunday evening service to begin. There weren't a lot of people in church that night. Looking around I saw maybe 20 people, all of whom I knew well.

Pale-skinned, fair-haired David sat at the piano. Carl—tall, black, basketball-playing Carl—stood at the front with Naomi, Pastor Andy's wife, and some others leading worship. From the front row, Jill, with her thick, dark hair and beautiful olive skin, flipped the overhead transparencies after each song. Floyd, the almost-blind man with eyes that never stopped jittering, was sitting in his usual chair, two rows back and two seats in from the left aisle.

Pastor Andy stepped to the podium to preach. He turned the well-worn pages of his brown, leather-bound King James Bible—the one he always used. As he read from Isaiah 53, that word once more confronted me.

> *Yet it pleased the* L*ORD to bruise him; he hath put him to grief: when thou shalt make his* ***soul*** *an offering for sin, he shall see his seed, he shall prolong his days, and the pleasure of the* L*ORD shall prosper in his hand. He shall see the travail of his* ***soul,*** *and shall be satisfied: by his knowledge shall my righteous servant justify many; for he shall bear their iniquities. Therefore will I divide him a portion with the great, and he shall divide the spoil with the strong; because he hath poured out his* ***soul*** *unto death* (Isaiah 53:10-12).

Soul. There was that word again.

Here was God the Father seeing the travail of His Son's *soul* and being satisfied. Here was Jesus pouring out His *soul* on the cross. Here was our Savior—the perfect Son of Man—offering up His *soul* for our sins.

Soul. Soul. Soul. What was it about that word? In my mind, it conjured up thoughts of something precious, mystical and sacred—something human, yet divine at the same time. Why was the soul such a vital part of who we were? What was the soul anyway?

Sitting on the metal folding chair that evening, my mind jumped back to scattered memories.

I had been a Christian for more than 30 years, but I couldn't recall any teaching or preaching on the soul. As a developmental psychologist, I had spent years studying the inner child, yet I knew almost nothing about that part; in fact, the soul wasn't even a construct recognized by the profession. And despite my recent study at the kitchen table, I still couldn't understand the concept of the soul.

Looking down at the Bible on my lap—a New American Standard Version—I reread the verses Andy had just quoted from Isaiah 53:

> *But the* L*ORD* *was pleased to crush Him, putting Him to grief; if He would render* ***Himself*** *as a guilt offering, He will see His offspring, He will prolong His days, and the good pleasure of the* L*ORD* *will prosper in His hand. As a result of the anguish of His* ***soul,*** *He will see it and be satisfied; by His knowledge the Righteous One, My Servant, will justify the many, as He will bear their iniquities. Therefore, I will allot Him a portion with the great, and He will divide the booty with the strong; because He poured out* ***Himself*** *to death.*

In a flash of understanding, I perceived it clearly. The words "His soul" in the King James is translated "Himself" in the New American Standard.

Jesus' soul was the essence of who He was. As the Son of Man who died on the cross, He offered up Himself—His soul—for our sins!

"Wow!" I thought. "Then my soul is the essence of myself—of whom God created me to be!"

I pictured Jesus standing before the synagogue worshipers in Nazareth. He had opened the scroll and read: *The Spirit of the Lord God is upon Me. . . . He has sent Me to heal the brokenhearted, to proclaim liberty to the captives, and the opening of the prison to those who are bound* (Isaiah 61:1).

Jesus came to bind up the brokenhearted, to liberate captives and to set prisoners free. But what did that mean? These things didn't automatically happen when we believed in Him for salvation. Neither did they refer to physical well-being of the body. These verses spoke of something more. Could it be something to do with the soul?

I looked around me at the people in the room. David was leaning back in his chair in the front row with his legs stretched out toward the pulpit. Carl was scribbling notes in his binder. Naomi was sitting on a padded green chair off to the side. From the back of the room, Jill listened, leaning up against a wall. Floyd was still seated in his same place—two chairs in from the outside aisle, second row from the front.

We were all just ordinary, struggling people, trying to be "good Christians"—trying to be kind to each other in the midst of all the problems. But where was the freedom and vibrant life promised us in Christ Jesus? More desperately than ever before, I wanted things right so I could be myself. I wanted the hidden places—within me, Jake, Dennis and others—healed. And I wanted the freedom to share God's love with people as He had created me to.

I had to understand what was going on deep within me—in my soul. Human knowledge of how to fix things on the outside could not repair the hurts nor remedy the ills that plagued my family and me from within. Doctors, counselors, psychologists and pastors—trained, professional and kind as they were—could not point me to the path leading to the cure for the inner sickness.

But I knew that God wanted to heal the problems that lay deep within us. He was the source of the love. He would cure the soul sickness. Jesus had paid the price for complete and total restoration of us.

I just didn't understand what He had already accomplished. And because I didn't understand, I didn't know how to let God bring the potential locked away within me to expression in the real world.

I had to know God in a more vast and vibrant way. I had to know Him as the Healer of the Brokenhearted and the Liberator of the Captives.

Somehow I had to let Him work deep within the essence of my humanity—in my soul.

CHAPTER 7

"Let Me In."

Despite limited understanding of my soul and its messed-up condition, God heard my cries for help and began healing me before I was even aware of the nature of the disease. Looking back on it now, I realize the love He'd given me had to permeate my soul before I could begin to live it out to the world. Way down in the core of myself, I had to believe in the love of God so that it could bubble forth freely from within.

But before God could get the love into my soul, He had to get the lies out. I had to let Him cleanse me of the twisted way of thinking I held in the deep recesses of my mind—in my soul.

The disease diagnosis was untruths buried deep in the soul. The treatment plan was the love of God.

Propelled onward by the continuing trials in my family and supported by church friends, I began to open up to God in a way I had never done before. Without knowing exactly what was occurring, I began allowing the Holy Spirit access to my damaged soul. Let me explain how it started for me.

In addition to being a pastor, Andy is also a licensed family counselor. We have prayer meetings in the front part of the church office, but in the back is a library and a counseling room.

Initially I went to counseling for the same reasons I came to the prayer meeting—family issues for which there seemed no solution. But we never talked about Jake or Dennis specifically. In fact, the sessions went nothing like I'd been taught in graduate school when studying various counseling theories such as Reality Therapy, Behavior Modification or Family Therapy. At the basis of these theories lay the assumption that changing some set of behaviors or conscious thoughts was enough to resolve the presenting problem.

The Christian marriage counselor Dennis and I had seen approached our issues in this way. Together the three of us had worked out some behavioral changes. Dennis would let me know when he would be home for dinner; if he was going to be late, he'd call. Dennis had also agreed to write me a letter or give me a card before he left on a trip. On my part, I had agreed to stop nagging and instead greet Dennis every evening with a kiss. By changing these external behaviors, it was hoped our relationship would improve.

But unlike these approaches, Andy took a step back and tried to ferret out the root cause of the deep thoughts and feelings driving the behaviors. The assumption was that the problems in our lives—the bad fruit—were rooted in misconceptions buried deep in the mind. Counseling hinged on the belief that solutions would come as we began believing the truth about God and ourselves.

As I understand it now, we humans were created with a universal need: God's love is essential to each one of us. We can't be the people God created us to be until we know how much He loves us. Every soul longs for the love of God. Without that, it will never be fulfilled.

But it's hard to believe in His love because from very early on, our minds are warped and we begin thinking that the heavenly Father's love is like that of our imperfect parents and other caregivers. Especially during traumatic moments in our babyhood, lies about ourselves, others and God get a foothold in our deep minds. From the core of our being, these lies speak to us: "No one loves me." "No one cares." We think, "God doesn't love me because . . ."

As we grow, these misconceptions become self-fulfilling prophecies; we come to understand ourselves, others and God in the context of the lie. Therefore, depending on the basic falsehood we believe, we may try and try to be perfect, give up in total confusion, punish ourselves and so on.

When we become Christians, these contaminated thoughts do not necessarily leave our deep mind. We learn Scripture, but that does not imply that we fully believe the verses we quote. When we accept Christ, we do not automatically see God as He really is. We do not spontaneously begin thinking about ourselves the way God thinks about us. Rather, the Bible encourages us to *be transformed by the renewing of your mind* (Romans 12:2).

Psalm 51 provides a clear framework for this sort of counseling. *Behold, I was brought forth in iniquity, and in sin my mother conceived me. Behold, You desire truth in the inward parts, and in the hidden part You will make me to know wisdom. . . . Create in me a clean heart, O God* (Psalm 51:5-6, 10).

We were conceived in sin and born with the mind of fallen Adam. But the Holy Spirit desires truth in our hidden parts. If we open ourselves to Him, He will lead us in exposing and eradicating the root lies that cause the harmful thoughts, feelings and behavioral patterns.

Simply and purely, this type of counseling involves trusting God's love enough to let Him in to heal the hidden framework of ourselves. It allows the Holy Spirit access to our souls so He can straighten our bent ways of thinking and impart the love truths of Christ.

Jesus was knocking on the door of my soul asking for an invitation to enter so He could do His work as the Counselor and Great Physician. He was pleading, "Let Me in." All He needed was for me to open my inner self to Him. Jesus is a gentleman. He never comes without first being invited.

And so I began starting each counseling session with a simple, desperate prayer: "Search me O God and know my heart. Try me and see if there be any way in me that is not Your way. I open myself to You, Lord. Please clean out the lies and replace them with Your truth. I trust You to do Your work in me today."

And week after week, slowly but surely, the lies and associated hurts peeled off like layers of an onion—like the wrappings of graveclothes. Let me give a specific example of something that happened soon after I began counseling.

One day I was in line at the grocery store checkout. I had already loaded the items from my cart onto the moving belt when I remembered I'd forgotten to get sliced Muenster cheese at the deli. So I went back to pick some up. It shouldn't have taken long, but it did. The clerk at the deli counter was new and didn't know how to work the scale.

I kept trying to hurry her along, but nothing helped. I felt anxious—way out of proportion to what the situation warranted. I mean, how much does it really matter if the cashier had to wait an extra two minutes to ring up my groceries? But I was stressed. "I've probably plugged up the checkout line," I thought. "People are waiting because of me. Somebody will get irritated. Time is precious and I'm wasting it. I'm not considering others. . . . I'm not being good."

My mini-panic/condemnation attack was off the chart in comparison to the emotions warranted by the actual event. That was the clue. In its exaggerated emotional response, my soul was crying out for help. It was as if a scab had been scraped off, and the unhealed wound beneath was bleeding profusely.

So I brought the event up at the next counseling session . . . and remembered a time in fifth grade.

We had moved to San Luis Obispo halfway through the year, and I'd started attending a new school. My teacher, Mrs. Manny, was a stickler for being on time. She also frequently raised her voice.

I hated being tardy. Being yelled at was even worse. So I would get in the car right after breakfast and wait for Mama to drive us to school, hoping that I wouldn't be late. But my little brother, Peter, didn't move fast in the mornings.

And so I was late . . . repeatedly. Mrs. Manny reprimanded me. I got detention. Once I tried to sneak in during the flag salute, but Mrs. Manny saw me and started yelling. As the "new girl" in class, I was humiliated in front of my new friends. I was doing something "wrong," and my teacher had pointed this out to the entire class. I'd been bad. Mrs. Manny was angry. My peers wouldn't accept me. Nobody would love me.

This downward spiral of my thoughts led to the core of the lie: People—and by projection, God—wouldn't love me because I had done something wrong.

With the lie exposed, Pastor Andy guided me to let Jesus replace it and the associated wrong emotions. In truth, Mrs. Manny didn't know why I was late. She responded out of ignorance of the facts and probably out of some lie in her past as well. And so I forgave her and believed the truth—that she would have expressed love to me if she'd been able to and that Jesus loves me regardless. He loves me despite my "right" or "wrong" behavior.

As time progressed, I began to realize that when I felt undue stress, anger, sadness or any other over-exaggerated, unhealthy emotional response, it was my soul shouting for help. I started seeing these emotions as warning flags and welcoming them as reminders to allow God access to the hurting part within. Once I realized this, much of the healing began to occur outside of formal "counseling" as I simply decided to give Jesus continued access to my soul.

With each passing week, deeper deceptions were exposed. Sometimes replacing the lies tore at the foundations of who I perceived myself to be. I wondered how I would now function without that particular false belief that had been such a part of me.

During one soul-healing encounter, I saw my good works—like writing papers about malnutrition in Africa or working for a mission organization—as a way to earn favor with people and God (so that I would be loved). Another time I realized how much of my doing things for Jake, Bryn, Anne, Mark and Dennis had been because of my insecurities; I needed to feel like a responsible parent/wife because being responsible was good and people would love me if I were good. In this sense, what I called "love" was really a form of self-centeredness; my "loving" behaviors fed my need to feel like a good person.

After seeing such tainted motivations in myself, all I could do was repent and ask God, and others whom I had hurt, for forgiveness.

As a child I had believed that if I did good things, my parents would love me, and if I did bad things, they wouldn't. And I'd projected this onto God and assumed the same of Him. Subtly, below the radar of my conscious thought, I'd believed, "Mary, God loves you, but He loves you more when you do good things and less when you do wrong." The other misconceptions I held were smaller rootlets springing from this bad taproot.

Exposing this lie and replacing it with the truth of God's unconditional love resulted in massive, paradigm-shifting change. I didn't think like I had before. I felt less stress—about always trying to do good things. Not being perfect didn't bother me as much. I didn't constantly judge myself and others. Rather than scrutinizing people, I just began enjoying them.

Sometimes I wondered if I could trust these changes, but I looked at the results in my life—love, joy, peace, patience, long-suffering—and realized that fruit doesn't lie. Good fruit cannot come from a bad tree (see Matthew 7:18).

Freedom was happening for me. Prison doors were opening. Scripture says, *And you shall know the truth, and the truth shall make you free* (John 8:32). Knowing how much God loved me was setting me free.

And an additional part of the truth I was coming to understand was how God had uniquely created us human beings to share the love He gave us with the world.

Part Three

Invisible Anatomy

Before I could more completely understand how God intended to solve the problem of why I did not love and my family difficulties, I first had to know how He had created me to function in the first place.

God made us in His image—as triune beings. He intends the spirit, soul and body to work together to allow His light, life and love to flow into us, through us and out of us to a dry and thirsty world.

But issues—in my soul especially—were blocking that flow.

CHAPTER 8

In His Image: Three-Part Beings

Looking back on it now, I couldn't lay hold of God's provision for the right way to live and love because I didn't know the truth of how God had designed us humans to function. This was an area I thought I knew something about. After all, I was a developmental psychologist, and both Dennis and my brother were physicians. But I was without understanding . . . until God's Word shed light and the pieces of the puzzle began to fall into place.

Our awesome God created us in His image. Scripture tells us, *Then God said, "Let Us make man in Our image, according to Our likeness." . . . So God created man in His own image; in the image of God He created him* (Genesis 1:26-27).

God is a triune God. He is Father, Son and Holy Spirit (see Matthew 28:19). And being fashioned after His design, we also are triune beings. Our three parts are spirit, soul and body.*

---

* All other components of our being that are spoken of in the Bible—such as the "mind," "flesh," "heart" and "will"—are either a combination of these three parts or a piece of them.

As a child in Sunday school, I had known of the triune nature of God and that we were created in His image. However, even as an adult sitting in the pew, I had not been explicitly aware of the three-part structure of humans. Yet Scripture is crystal-clear: *And the LORD God formed man of the dust of the ground, and breathed into his nostrils the breath of life; and man became a living soul* (Genesis 2:7, KJV).

God shaped Adam's *body* from the elements of the earth. Then He breathed His life into man's nostrils. He blew His Spirit—His very Self—into the body so that Adam, too, had a *spirit.* And with that breath, man became alive. He became himself—a living *soul.*

God formed our outside covering of organs, bones and flesh from the earth. That is the part we call the body; it is the container for the inner hidden parts of soul and spirit. The *body* allows us to live and function in the physical world.

Then God breathed into that body His breath of life. God is a Spirit, and He breathed into Adam His life-giving Spirit. The same Spirit of God who moved over the surface of the waters in creation came into man. By God's Spirit-breath, Adam became alive. When we accept Christ, our *spirit* is made alive by His indwelling Spirit.

Upon receiving that breath of Spirit-life into his body, Adam became a "living soul." In some translations, these words are translated "living being." To put it another way, when God's Spirit entered into him, man became himself—a person with his own individual way of thinking, feeling and reacting. The *soul* is our inner framework—our personality.

The three-part structure of us humans is described in the New Testament as well. In 1 Thessalonians 5:23, Paul says, *Now may the God of peace Himself sanctify you completely; and may your whole* ***spirit, soul,*** *and* ***body*** *be preserved blameless at the coming of our Lord Jesus Christ.*

In initially grasping the concept of how God made us as three-part beings, it helped me to think of myself as a garden hose. In this simplified comparison, the spirit is the screw-on part that connects the hose with the faucet; the spirit joins us to God, our source of living water. The soul is represented by the long, flexible part that directs the flow of water. And the body is like the sprinkler at the end; through it, water sprays out and brings life to the earth.

In order for water to flow through a garden hose, all three parts must work properly. Imagine a watering system with a bent faucet attachment, a kink in the rubber hose or a sprinkler clogged with dirt and debris. A problem in any part will prevent water from traveling from the source to the dry place.

Just as with the parts of a garden hose, the spirit, soul and body are meant to work together in alignment and agreement. In this way, the love of God flows into us (via our spirits), through us (via our souls) and out of us (via our bodies) to the world.

But in reality, God connects with us—dwells or unites with us—in the center of our beings. He comes first to our deadened spirit and makes it alive in Him. From there His life radiates out—to the soul, the body and the world.

As I pondered this, a different analogy—one of a lighthouse—came to mind. At the center of the lighthouse is a light source—a flame or an electric bulb. Mirrors positioned carefully at various angles surround the light source. If they are kept clean, polished and properly angled, they reflect and magnify the brilliance of the light. The tower protects the light source and the mirrors, providing a structure from which the light can shine out, warning passing ships of danger.

In the lighthouse analogy, the flame (representing the spirit), the mirrors (representing the soul) and the tower (representing the body) are all vital. They work together in allowing the inner light—God within—to illuminate the world.

To personalize these analogies, I have a *spirit* that connects me to God. When I accepted Christ, it became alive. God is in me, and I relate to Him spirit-to-Spirit.

With my *body* I breathe air, eat food and live on the earth. The body is the outward housing that allows my inward parts of spirit and soul to have a place of residence on earth.

My *soul* is who I really am—my personality. It includes my thought processes, my desires and my emotional reactions. It is the framework that determines how I think of and behave toward myself, God and others. God within me passes through this framework of my humanity before He becomes visible to the world.

In God's perfect design, the Holy Spirit in our spirit brings Himself to our soul and body as well. In this way, God provides everything we need to function in the world as He created us to. With God as the source and supply in our spirit and with our soul and body falling into alignment with that, we come alive with Him and carry His essence—His light, life and love—to others.

The glory of God is man fully alive, wrote Saint Irenaeus around A.D. 185. I agree! When we let God make us completely alive in all three parts, we will express His glory for all the world to see. God created us so that His love could flow into us (via our spirits), flow through us (via our souls) and flow out of us (via our bodies).

God intended for me to function as a conduit of Himself. He would get me to loving. He would lead me along the path of healing for me and my family.

But before I could grasp the completed work of Christ for the cure, I first had to understand more of how God intended the three parts of me to work individually . . . and how I had deviated from His plan.

CHAPTER 9

Our Spirit: The Life Within

From my early days in Sunday school, I knew some rather vague truths about the spirit. I knew that prior to accepting Christ, we are spiritually dead. Eternal life begins the moment we invite Him in. I understood that if you are a true Christian, God lives in you. When we "accept Jesus," the Holy Spirit comes and dwells in us. The phrase "Christ lives in me" (see Galatians 2:20) refers to this.

As a Christian I had understood these truths, but until the trials in my life pushed me deeper, I had never asked the obvious question: When I accept Christ, what part of me does the Holy Spirit actually indwell? Now I understand that the Holy Spirit comes to live in my spirit. When I invited Jesus into my heart, the Holy Spirit came in and enlivened my spirit. God is a spirit so we connect to Him Spirit-to-spirit.

In Old Testament times, God resided in the inner chamber of the temple called the Holy of Holies. In the New Testament, our bodies are called the temple, and our spirit—the innermost chamber of our temple—is the habitation of God's Spirit on earth.

With my spirit, I am connected to God's life-giving Spirit. Scripture tells us, *It is the Spirit who gives life; the flesh profits nothing* (John 6:63). We are made alive by union with Christ in our spirit.

When I accepted Christ, my spirit became alive in new birth so that I could communicate with God. By our spirits we know and perceive God and live in continuous life-giving relationship with Him. The Holy Spirit enlightens us through union with our human spirit. Romans 8:16 says, *The Spirit Himself bears witness with our spirit that we are children of God.*

It's actually very simple. Our spirit connects us to the spiritual realm much as our body connects us to the physical realm. Just as the body has senses that connect us with the physical world, the spirit has senses that connect us with the spiritual world. Just as our bodies are meant to know the stuff of earth, our spirits are meant to know the stuff of heaven.

The spirit's organs of perception operate by faith, "not by sight." Some of the senses of the spirit that keep us in touch with God are spiritual sight (with "eyes of the heart") and hearing (with "spiritual ears").

For instance, we might have a dream or see a vision of what God is doing. We might hear in our spirits a word of knowledge for someone or a prompting to do something God wants done. We also may feel something of what the Lord is feeling when we groan in prayer. It is through our spirits that we perceive and know the thoughts, emotions and will of God.

In Jesus, we see God's perfect plan for how our spirits should operate. As a child, Jesus *grew and became strong in spirit* (Luke 2:40). It does not say that His body or soul became strong. This is vitally important; Jesus' spirit connection with God, not influences from His body or soul, defined and energized Him as a man who walked this earth.

Jesus grew "strong in spirit" by exercising His spirit and staying tuned into God. Jesus lived in continuous union with the Father. He saw what His

Father was doing and heard what His Father was saying by perceiving these things in His spirit. Jesus' human spirit and the Holy Spirit enjoyed unbroken fellowship.

This connection enabled Jesus to speak only what the Father gave Him to say. He said, *For I have not spoken on My own authority; but the Father who sent Me gave Me a command, what I should say and what I should speak. And I know that His command is everlasting life. Therefore, whatever I speak, just as the Father has told Me, so I speak* (John 12:49-50).

Jesus did only what He saw the Father doing. He said, *The Son can do nothing of Himself, but what He sees the Father do* (John 5:19). Everything Jesus spoke or did came from God through His spirit.

I also began to realize that Jesus not only understood what God wanted Him to do by way of His spirit, but through His spirit He also received the power to do it. Jesus walked on water and healed the sick. He cast out demons and turned water into wine. The supernatural ability to do these things came from God—through the perfect Spirit-to-spirit connection Jesus had with His Father. Jesus healed out of compassion (see Luke 7:13, 10:33, 15:20). That compassion came from the Father's love.

With this monumental understanding came the realization that just as it was in Jesus, God's Son, so it is also supposed to be in us, His adopted sons and daughters. Our spirits were made by God for the purpose of keeping us in constant relationship with Him. Via the connection the Holy Spirit has with our spirits, we are meant to know God and draw on Him as Jesus did.

Jesus prayed for us, . . . *that they all may be one, as You, Father, are in Me and I in You; that they also may be one in Us* (John 17:21). Jesus wants us to be in unbroken union with the Father just as He was.

Our spirits are of heavenly essence—the substance of God. They speak the language of God. We relate directly to God on a vertical plane, His

Spirit with our spirit—Spirit-to-spirit. *God is Spirit, and those who worship Him must worship in spirit and truth* (John 4:24).

God is the source. His Spirit comes into my spirit and makes me alive. But in order for others to see the Holy Spirit in me, the light, life and love of God in my spirit has to be let out to the world.

To relate to people as God intended, I have to communicate with them person-to-person on a horizontal plane. I shake their hands. I speak kind words they can understand. However, I don't do that type of relating with my spirit. I do that with my soul as it expresses itself via my body. In God's design, even though we relate to people and the things of this world with our souls and bodies, we do that in the union with Him provided through our spirits.

Consider for instance the verse, *If we* ***live*** *in the Spirit, let us also* ***walk*** *in the Spirit* (Galatians 5:25). We were meant to *live*—to have eternal life by His Spirit—and also to *walk* the road of life communicating His life and love to the world by His Spirit. That is, we *live* and *walk* with guidance and energy supplied by the Holy Spirit through union with our spirit.

Over and over again in the New Testament we are encouraged to do things such as worship, move, be fervent, be resolved in purpose and so on, "in the Spirit" (for example, see John 4:23-24). We were created to do everything by union with His Spirit in our spirit enlivening the whole being of us.

God's life in us is not supposed to stay boxed up in our spirits. It is to extend to our soul and body as well. A king lives in a castle, but his rulership is meant to extend beyond that place of residence to the entire kingdom.

I understand now that God wants my whole being to be energized by the Holy Spirit. When I had accepted Christ at age 16, that wasn't supposed to be only a transaction whereby I gave assent to Jesus' residence in my spirit. When God entered into me that day, I became a totally new creation so I could live with every fiber of my humanity filled to overflowing with Him.

God may have already given you a clear understanding of this, but because I had been unaware of how the spirit part of me was designed, I had made some grievous errors.

As a teenager up in the hills behind the apple orchard with Degan, Sunshine and my Bible, I had begun as God intended. In that beautiful simplicity, I was learning to live out of my connection to God. But once the unhurried times of meditation in the hills faded into the busy years of college study and beyond, my fellowship with God faded too. I did not know enough to give time and place to spiritual development in this way, so my spirit atrophied like an unexercised muscle.

I also did not understand that my vertical Spirit-to-spirit connection to God was to be the source for living out God's life and love in horizontal relationships with others. Good and right as those times in the hills were, there was a lot more to loving than shouting, "Jesus, I love you," into the wild, sage-tinged air.

In God's design, those hills were to be a learning ground for unity with Him that would sustain me in the world of people and problems. By allowing God's Spirit to enliven my spirit *and my soul and body as well,* God's love in me could bring life and healing to every person I met. But because I didn't understand this, I hadn't allowed Him access to my whole person.

His love had poured into me that night on the floor of the church, but that love had stayed jailed up in my spirit. I had said, "I surrender all" and I'd let Him have all that I knew to give. But I hadn't given Him the soul part of myself. I hadn't known to believe for more because I didn't understand how God had created me so that all three parts worked together to radiate His life and love.

What good is a million dollars if you can't spend it? What good is love if you can't share it with others? Love isn't love until you give it away.

To love others as God designed, our bodies and souls must also be aligned with His plan.

CHAPTER 10

Our Body: The Temple

The body is the outward covering for the inner parts of spirit and soul. It allows the spirit and soul to have a dwelling place on earth. The Bible tells us, *Your body is the temple of the Holy Spirit* (1 Corinthians 6:19).

The body is the part of us we see with our earthly eyes. Our bodies were created by God to be maintained by sustenance from the physical world. We eat what grows on the earth and breathe its air.

Just as the spirit lives with eternal life via its connection to heaven, the body lives with physical life via its connection to the earth. The spirit of man is made of the stuff of the spiritual realm; our bodies were formed from the dust of the earth and are of the physical realm. Just as the spirit is our window to God, the body is our window to the world. The body is the part of us whereby we know and interact with the stuff of earth. When physical life leaves the body, the spirit and soul no longer have a place of residence on earth.

But while we are here, we receive input from the physical world through our body's five senses. We see, hear, smell, taste and feel. It is as natural and right to interact with the physical realm with our bodies as it is to interact with the spiritual realm with our spirits.

Up in the hills with Degan and Sunshine, my body was every bit as alive as my spirit. I would watch a cottontail bounce through the grass and listen to quail rustling in the underbrush. I'd wade in a cool stream and taste the wild blackberries that grew on its banks. The smell of sage and horse mixed together drifted lazily in the air as I lay in the shade reading my Bible.

Jesus was beautifully in tune to the world in which He lived. In His parables, He drew spiritual realities from physical ones. He saw golden fields of grain and told stories of farmers sowing seeds on different types of soil and of wheat and weeds growing up together. He was aware of how vineyards grew and related that to our spiritual lives. He noticed fig trees and lilies, birds and mustard seeds, sheep and goats.

Jesus was perfectly aware of both the spiritual *and* earthly realms. His whole life was about making invisible, spiritual God manifest in physical reality. In Christ, *the Word became flesh and dwelt among us, and we beheld His glory* (John 1:14). The Father wanted to communicate His love to humanity, but we, having shut ourselves off from God through the Fall, couldn't understand Him. Our spirits were dead; we didn't speak His heavenly language. So He sent His Son to express love in a human life we could see with our physical eyes and relate to person-to-person.

And today God intends that the world see Christ in us—as our bodies radiate the glory of God.

The body part of us is incredibly valued by God. Without our bodies, there would be no visible expression of Christ in us for the world to see. Our bodies were designed as vessels—like lighthouse towers—to carry His light, life and love to the world. Second Corinthians 4:7 says, *But we have this treasure in earthen vessels, that the excellence of the power may be of God and not of us.*

God made the "earthen vessels" to display His handiwork. The glory of God is meant to shine out through our bodies even more so than it shone from the face of Moses (see 2 Corinthians 3:7-10). The eternal life in our spirits is meant to fill our souls and pour out through our bodies to the world.

The body is not evil. God created even the flesh of us to be good. He designed the life of Jesus to be visible in our body. Second Corinthians 4:11 says, . . . *that the life of Jesus also may be manifested in our mortal flesh.*

"Flesh," meaning the meat on our bones, is as much a part of God's excellent creation as are our spirits and souls. (The term "in the flesh" refers to something else entirely and will be discussed in Chapter 20, "Strivings of the Soul.")

Scripture encourages us to present our bodies as a "living sacrifice." *I beseech you therefore, brethren, by the mercies of God, that you present your bodies a living sacrifice, holy, acceptable to God, which is your reasonable service* (Romans 12:1). God wants the living sacrifice of our bodies so that He can energize our entire humanity (not just our spirits) with the life of Christ.

But I had misinterpreted Romans 12:1 and thought that my body was fundamentally flawed and needed to be done away with. I had then made the additional mistake of trying to accomplish that sacrifice myself—by stamping sin out of my body using my own methods.

This wrong thinking was reflected in the way I dealt with myself for most of my Christian life. I attempted to smash sin out of my body. I tried and then asked God for strength to try harder, to curb wrongness in myself by putting on the shiny armor of "proper Christian" behaviors.

But the exercise, discipline and punishment only resulted in a façade that looked commendable on the surface. What came from my body did not emanate from the core of myself where God lived. It did not spring from a rightness and purity within. Rather, it came from harsh external rules I imposed on myself to try to keep the sin suppressed so that I appeared Christlike.

In actuality, the shiny armor only filled me with pride. I thought *I* was good and that *I* had played a praiseworthy role in getting myself there.

But a proper-looking exterior is not what God is after.

The Bible warns of the futility of trying in our own efforts to make ourselves acceptable to God: *Why . . . do you subject yourselves to regulations—"Do not touch, do not taste, do not handle"? . . . These things indeed have an appearance of wisdom in self-imposed religion, false humility, and neglect of the body, but are of no value against the indulgence of the flesh* (Colossians 2:20-23). But somehow I had missed this warning.

I assumed it was possible for the good in me to cast out the bad. So I tried to fix myself by imposing more rules and regulations. I set a strict standard and judged myself (and others) by this high mark.

But now I understand that the Bible encourages us to present our bodies as "*living* sacrifices" so He can deal with the issues and make us right through and through.

Crucifixion is not a death one can accomplish alone; nobody ever committed suicide by crucifixion. It is not physically possible to pound nails into your own hands. But without realizing it, I had attempted to do just that. Rather than present a *living* sacrifice, I'd been trying to play God, accomplish the work of the cross and stamp evil out of myself.

I thought that if I worked hard enough, I could make what came out of me look commendable. And I assumed that if I looked good on the outside, I must really be good on the inside. So I kept on trying to make myself acceptable in this way.

The Pharisees made a similar mistake; Jesus called them "whitewashed tombs" (see Matthew 23:27). Life doesn't come from tombs.

Life and love only come from God. He wants His life inside of me to bubble forth. I wasn't made to function with my spirit in life-giving connection with God but with my body operating apart from Him—under "self control." Instead, I needed to understand God's provision for getting the life of the Spirit inside of me out to the world.

I had much to learn about the soul, through which the life and love of God were meant to flow.

CHAPTER 11

OUR SOUL: THE BRIDGE

From the time I had accepted Jesus back in high school, I'd understood something about the spirit and body parts of myself. I knew that the Holy Spirit lived in me, and therefore my spirit was alive. I also believed that my body was the temple of the Holy Spirit yet was prone to sin.

But I knew almost nothing about the soul. I never remember hearing any teaching or preaching about it. In church, some people used the terms "spirit," "heart" and "soul" interchangeably. Others didn't talk about it. Somewhere, though, I had memorized Watchman Nee's generally accepted definition: *The soul is the seat of the mind, the will and the emotions.* But I really didn't acknowledge my soul as a vital part of myself.

As I sought understanding of the nature and function of the soul, it became obvious that authors and theologians disagreed and that their definitions were unclear and often contradictory. My first working definition of the soul was "whatever is in us excluding spirit and body." It took months of meditating upon Scripture and researching Greek and Hebrew meanings, Bible encyclopedias, books and articles before I began to understand the concept of the soul.

But as I see it now, the soul is the part that defines our unique personality. Watchman Nee's classic definition is solid. The soul holds the mind, will and emotions that define us as human beings. Now when I see the words "mind," "will" or "emotions," I know these are part of the soul.

In the way that God created us, the soul is who we are—our character. Our soul is the house of our thoughts and beliefs from which come the distinctive motivations, emotions, words and actions that make us our unique selves. As such, a person *has* a body and a person *has* a spirit, but a person *is* his soul. The soul defines the person. The soul is the self. My soul is who I am. Your soul is who you are.

But the Bible also refers to the "heart." If we are composed of three parts—spirit, soul and body—then what is this important part called the "heart"?

What Scripture calls the "heart" is the inner part composed of both the spirit and the soul. The spirit is part of the heart (see, for example, 1 Peter 3:4) and so also is the soul (see, for example, 1 Peter 1:22). Both spirit and soul are closely knit together in the heart. Hebrews 4:12 says, *For the word of God is living and powerful, and sharper than any two-edged sword, piercing even to the division of soul and spirit, and of joints and marrow, and is a discerner of the thoughts and intents of the heart.*

In God's design of the heart, the spirit and the soul are to be perfectly aligned and intertwined. God intends for our hearts to be pure—full of God in both spirit and soul. When our soul lends its allegiance to the spirit and welcomes into itself all of God, the heart is pure and we live as God designed.

Our spirit contains God's Spirit and interacts with the spiritual realm. Our body interacts with the world—the physical realm. Our soul stands as the bridge between these two realms. It serves as a link between them.

The soul has free will. It decides how the person operates. Will the soul be led by the spirit (as directed by God), or will the soul opt to follow its own autonomous leading? The soul does not have to bend its knee to the spirit. If the soul—the "I"—resists, the Holy Spirit (through our spirit) will not force His will.

Based on the core beliefs it harbors within itself, the soul determines what we do and how we act. Will the soul come into agreement with the Spirit, or will it make its own decisions and act autonomously? Will the man or woman be ruled by the puffed-up "I" of his or her soul or by the surrendered "I" conformed to the spirit's leading? This is the monumental question of our lives.

In this way, the soul makes continual choices that come to define our lives as human beings. What should we do at any moment? Sleep, pray, mow the lawn, watch TV? And with what underlying attitude will the action be done? With resentment, resolve, joy, love? Based on deep core structures of belief, the soul determines these decisions, moment by moment throughout each day.

It is in the soul—in the inner framework of the person—that the will resides. And what the soul wills, the body carries out. The soul puts a smile on our face and lights us up with joy at seeing an old friend. Of course we can put on a fake smile and fool people, maybe even ourselves, for a while, but God knows the truth of what's inside.

The mind, will and emotions determine the attitudes and actions that express themselves out through the body. Our behaviors, speech and many of the infirmities of our bodies are simply outward expressions of the inward soul. The soul leads and the body follows.

Romans 12:2 says, *And do not be conformed to this world, but be transformed by the renewing of your mind, that you may prove what is that good and acceptable and perfect will of God.* When our mind (in our soul) is transformed by the truth of Christ, that is expressed out through our body. The perfect will of God shows itself to the world when the will of God, taken into our soul, is manifest in the body.

Ephesians 4:23-24 says, *Be made new in the attitude of your minds; and . . . put on the new self, created to be like God* (NIV). "The new self created to be like God" comes from a renewed mind.

Whatever is in the soul—good or evil, naughty or nice—will come out through the body. The body allows the outward expression of the mind, will and emotions. It is the content of our soul, not our spirit directly, that causes us to act as we do and be the people that we are.

We may hide our true selves for a while by dressing the body in the polished armor of commendable behaviors, but the unhealed parts of our soul will eventually find a crack, slip out and manifest themselves in awful behaviors that we cannot believe even came from ourselves. That's why an affair slipped out of me—something I would never have guessed was possible. Deep inside of me, my soul wasn't right. It believed crippling lies, causing unmet needs and deep hurts, that eventually burst forth in ugly ways.

But in God's design, the eternal life in my spirit is meant to wash my soul clean as it conforms itself to the will of God. The spirit is to gently guide, and the soul is to willingly bend its knee to that guidance. In this way, the body comes to function properly, not by putting external rules on it (like I had tried to do), but by letting the God-filled spirit guide the soul.

In God's perfect way, His life in our spirit, taken into the core of who we are—in our souls—is expressed out through our body. God thus enlivens our personality, transforming us into our true selves. In this way, we live in love relationship with Him and others as His love pours through us.

Tall, basketball-playing Carl first helped me to see that love for others has to pass through our souls. I'd been talking about the soul in Sunday school for several weeks, and the whole class was getting involved. One day, Carl shared about David and Jonathan: *Now when he had finished speaking to Saul, the* ***soul*** *of Jonathan was knit to the* ***soul*** *of David, and Jonathan loved him as his own* ***soul*** (1 Samuel 18:1).

"David and Jonathan were best friends," Carl told me. "They loved each other soul-to-soul."

It was revelation to him and to me. We love others with our souls!

I began to see this truth elsewhere in Scripture as well. In the Song of Solomon (NASB), the Shulamite woman loves the king with her soul: *Tell me, O you whom my* ***soul*** *loves* (1:7). *On my bed night after night I sought him whom my* ***soul*** *loves* (3:1). *I must seek him whom my* ***soul*** *loves* (3:2).

God wants us to love others from a pure heart—one in which the soul is aligned with the spirit and in agreement with God. First Peter 1:22 says, *Since you have purified your souls in obeying the truth through the Spirit in sincere love of the brethren, love one another fervently with a pure heart.*

We can't love others with the spirit alone. We need the soul—the human element. We love and interact with others primarily through our souls. In some circles, the phrase "soulical love" is used with negative connotations. But there is nothing wrong and everything right with soulical love *when the soul is guided by the spirit.* We love others as God designed by letting His love in our spirits fill our souls.

To me, that made it crystal-clear that the problem Edna had pointed out—of me not loving—lay with issues in my soul. My deep mind was contaminated with twisted thinking that prevented the love of God in me from flowing out. In the core of myself, I didn't believe in the love of God.

The problem wasn't in my spirit; it was alive in Christ. I knew the love of God in my spirit. The problem wasn't in my body either; it just followed the leading of my soul. The problem of my not loving was in my soul. In addition, the affair that haunted me, along with Jake's and Dennis' issues, were symptoms of sick souls.

How could I have studied biology and psychology among the hundreds of thousands of volumes in Cubberly Library at Stanford and not seen these vitally important principles about human function? How could I have written articles detailing the latest research on the mind and behavior at UCLA's Neuropsychiatric Institute, with soul issues staring me in the face, and not know these fundamentals? How could I have gone to church and read the Bible for more than 40 years and missed God's basic design of humanity?

I had bought into lies planted by "the enemy of our souls" and common to all mankind. Without conscious awareness of my soul and its proper functioning under leadership of the spirit, I had let my soul lead. But because I'd let it guide me with the principles I'd learned in church, I thought I was doing what God wanted. I thought that keeping myself in line with God's Word by encasing myself in an armor of Bible-based rules to hold the sins contained pleased God.

At the time, I subconsciously believed this armor served a useful purpose. I assumed it (1) prevented the yuck in me from coming out and (2) protected me from hurt—from the pain of things not being right, like with the Down's syndrome twins at UCLA or with Jake and Dennis.

But now I see that the walls were really a way of devaluing my soul. They were a way of saying, "Soul, I don't like you. I'm afraid of what comes out of you. So I'm locking you up in solitary confinement. I'm not going to pay attention to your cries for help. I'm not going to listen to what you really want."

By ignoring the soul and confining it in this way, I believed I was pleasing God. But really I was sabotaging myself—committing soul-suicide.

The armor I thought prevented the yuck from coming out and the hurt from coming in actually prevented the love of God from flowing. Without realizing it, I was blocking the life and love of God in my spirit from flooding into my soul and bubbling forth in joy, power and freedom. The living water was in me, but I'd dammed up its flow. Few things are as putrid and disease-breeding as stagnant water.

But now I know better. My soul—my personality—is God's precious gift to me. I am God's gift to me! He made my unique personality. I am perfectly suited to me! Despising the person He made is like scorning that gift. Trying to kill off my soul and then covering up the deadness with a show of nice deeds is like shattering the gift and then gluing it back together again in a shape that doesn't fit God's design and isn't capable of fulfilling His purpose.

God wants me to stop playing God and just love the gift He gave me. I do that by giving the gift of myself—my soul—back to Him with unabandoned honesty and confidence, regardless of how messed up I know myself to be. Then He can clean me with the pure infusion of His Word into my soul—from the inside out—and enliven my humanity.

One of the quotes I have copied into the front of my Bible says, *When we let God wake up our humanity, we will find that we are 1,000 times greater than ourselves.*

We were created to be great men and women of God.

That will happen when the spirit, soul and body come to function in perfect agreement with each other and with God.

CHAPTER 12

All Together Now: United Man

God designed all three parts of us humans to work together in unity to glorify Him.

Early in my understanding of this, I was trying to explain a jumbled version of how we are to function to the Sunday school class when Jill, with the thick, black hair, raised her hand.

"If it's God, it has to be simple," she said. "If it's too complicated to understand, it isn't God—or else it's a cloudy picture of God and we aren't seeing Him like He really is."

Jill's words have been a guiding principle for me as I've let these truths settle into their beautiful simplicity. It is not my intent to fill your mind with theories, analogies or theology but rather, to shed light on the simple truth so that we can be the people God created us to be.

Figure 12 helps me understand how we were made to function. In the illustration, the solid arrows pointing to the right and connecting the parts represent God giving Himself to us. Light, life and love come to us from God. **God is light;** Jesus said, *I am the light of the world* (John 8:12). God comes first as light (see Genesis 1:3). That light brings life (see Genesis 1:11, 20). **God is life;** Jesus said, *I am the bread of life* (John 6:35). Then God loves that which has life. First John 4:16 says, ***God is love.***

God's light comes to us in our spiritual darkness. If we turn to that **light,** we become alive with His spiritual **life.** Once we are alive, we can begin our **love** relationship with Him. When we are alive with His life, He can love us as He designed from the beginning—up close and personal. And we who have received God's love can then love others.

Love is His original and ultimate intent. It is the culmination of all He wants to share with the world. *For God **so loved the world** that He gave His only begotten Son . . .* (John 3:16).

God wants to give us His light, life and love. He came to make us lights. Jesus tells us, *You are the **light** of the world* (Matthew 5:14). He came to give us life: *I have come that they may have **life,** and that they may have it more abundantly* (John 10:10). And He came to love us so we could share that love with others: *A new commandment I give to you, that you **love** one another; as I have loved you, that you also **love** one another* (John 13:34).

The arrows in the figure thus represent God's inflow of Himself—His light, life and love and all the goodness those entail. When flowing through us, the goodness of God enters our spirit, passes through our soul and then floods out through our body. Of course in reality man is not linear, but multidimensional. God lives in the center of us—in our spirit—and radiates out from there, to the soul, the body, others and the world.

Note from the diagram that two realms—the spiritual and the physical—exist in this universe.*

---

* There is actually a soulical realm too. It is the environment of the mind, will and emotions—the milieu in which our soul functions. But its discussion is not necessary here.

The *spiritual* realm is the reality we experience with our spirit. It is the milieu of God's heavenly kingdom—the habitat of the Spirit. It is the environment of my connection with God.

The *physical* realm is the reality we experience in living on this earth. It is the world in which our bodies live and function. The hills behind the house where I grew up are part of this physical realm. So also are the masses of humanity on the dirty Mumbai streets. The earthly realm is the milieu in which our body resides.

Note from the figure that humans function in both the spiritual and physical realms. No other created being lives simultaneously in both. In this respect, God made us unique among all His creation—to be the link between heaven and earth.

People—not animals nor angels—were made for this purpose. Animals were created for earth. They have souls and bodies (see Psalm 104:28, 30) but lack spirits that connect them to God. Angels, on the other hand, are spiritual beings created for the spiritual realm; they have no physical bodies.

But we are simultaneously of the dust of the earth (like the fish and the birds) and of spirit (like the angels). As such, our spirit functions in the spirit realm, our body functions in the earthly realm and our soul stands in the middle between the two. The soul of man is the only part of God's creation that bridges the gap between these two realms.

In this sense, God made mankind alone to be the mediator between Himself and earth. We are perfectly fashioned to carry His light, life and love to earth.

God is love, and He wants to share that love with the world He created. But God is a Spirit, and the world is earthly. So how does God share Himself, who is spiritual, with the physical? He chooses to interact with the physical universe through human beings—whom He created to function in both realms.

We relay to others the Spirit life of God by expressing that life out through our physical body. When we interact with people or relate to the world, we don't do that with the spirit part of us. We do that with our physical bodies (through speech, touch, seeing, etc.). And how we do that is determined in our soul; it needs God's life and love to function as intended.

A passage from 1 Corinthians makes this clear. (In reading these verses, it helps to remember that the mind is in the soul.)

> *For if I pray in a tongue, my spirit prays, but my mind is unfruitful. What is the outcome then? I will pray* ***with the spirit*** *and I will pray* ***with the mind*** *also; I will sing* ***with the spirit*** *and I will sing* ***with the mind*** *also. Otherwise if you bless in the spirit only, how will the one who fills the place of the ungifted say the "Amen" at your giving of thanks, since he does not know what you are saying?* (1 Corinthians 14:14-16, NASB).

Although this Scripture is talking about prayer or singing, the principle applies to how we relate to God and to our fellow man in general. We communicate with God Spirit-to-spirit via our spirit, but we relate to people soul-to-soul via our mind, will and emotions, as expressed through our body.

As Carl had seen in Sunday school that day, we love others with our souls. In the soul, the love language of heaven—the love of God in our spirit—is translated into the love language of earth. This translation is necessary because we can't behold the love of God unless it is communicated in a language we understand. *The Word became flesh and dwelt among us* (John 1:14) so we could know God's love in visible, tangible form. God designed that we would know His love here and now on earth through each other.

As I've slowly come to realize, God's love pours into our spirit in one form, but it pours out from the body in another form. The *form* of the love changes in the soul.

Thinking of the vertical and horizontal beams of the cross helps me picture this. Jesus had a vertical love connection with the Father. His spirit was connected to God. Jesus also had a horizontal love connection with others. On the cross, His arms were spread wide to embrace the world.

The transposition from the vertical to the horizontal beams happens at the center of the cross—at the center of who we are—in the soul. What comes down from God in our vertical relationship to Him is an ungraspable, ethereal love having no concrete form like the little drops of liquid love that poured down on me that night in church. But when it passes through our soul, God's love takes on the shape of flesh-and-blood servanthood. It feeds the poor. It visits the sick. It hugs the dying.

So the *form* of the love—the language of it—changes in the soul. In the soul, love cloaks itself in frail humanity; it puts on humility. But although the *form* of the love changes, the *substance* of the love—the essence of it—does not.

In this sense, the love of God in heaven and the love of God seen on earth through others are like steam and water. Both are of the same substance. Both are H_2O. But steam, as a vaporous substance of the air, isn't much good to our bodies on earth. It can be harnessed as power, but it doesn't cool the tongue. It can't be played in or used to clean the body. It doesn't support life. Giving a cup of steam to a thirsty child doesn't work. In the soul, however, powerful, ethereal steam condenses into life-giving water. In the soul, love in its heavenly form condenses into the love that caresses the world.

And so we can say of the Son of Man's love, "Aha, yes, I see it." We relate to Jesus' form of love—that which walked the dusty roads of earth, healed the blind, fed the hungry and died on a rugged cross.

You and I were created so that others would know God's love as it is lived out in us. Jesus gave us some examples of what the love He wants us to share with the world looks like. He said,

> *I was hungry and you gave Me food; I was thirsty and you gave Me drink; I was a stranger and you took Me in; I was naked and you clothed Me; I was sick and you visited Me; I was in prison and you came to Me. . . . Inasmuch as you did it to one of the least of these My brethren, you did it to Me* (Matthew 25:35-36, 40).

We humans get to express God's heavenly, ethereal love in tangible, concrete ways. His heavenly love in an earthly form is meant to pour out of us. When we share His love with others, we are loving both God and others like He designed us to.

And that love of others—loving with God's love in our souls—is to be our mark of authenticity as Christians. Jesus said, *By this all will know that you are My disciples, if you have love for one another* (John 13:35). Love flowing through us to others is our mark of life! *We know that we have passed from death to life, because we love the brethren* (1 John 3:14).

As I realize it now, having God's love in my spirit alone simply isn't enough. We can be beautifully connected Spirit-to-spirit with God but still have tainted souls that hinder expression of God's love soul-to-soul with others.

I had known God's love in my spirit from the time I'd accepted Christ at age 16. I'd experienced more of that great love years later as I lay on the floor at the front of the church. But that love, great as it was, didn't saturate the substance of myself. It didn't come into my soul, purify it and flow out from deep within me because I didn't know to let God work in this way.

In fact, only recently have I come to understand that God created us humans to be fully alive in spirit, soul and body. He created us to translate the love language of heaven into the love language of earth!

However, "the enemy of our souls" does not want us awakening to this truth, stepping into our God-created, original formation and fulfilling our destiny. Using sordid schemes, he fights desperately to keep us from the love of God in any way he can.

Knowing how God created man, Satan sought to ruin each of the three parts so they could not function as designed. Through his dark plot, he attempted to unmake the spirit, the body and the soul in subtle ways so that we were undone but didn't know it.

If I were to be the person God had created me to be and live out Jesus' One Command to love others as He loved me, I had to understand how Satan had spoiled the human race.

I needed a deeper understanding of what happened to Adam and Eve in the Garden of Eden.

FIGURE 12

UNITED MAN

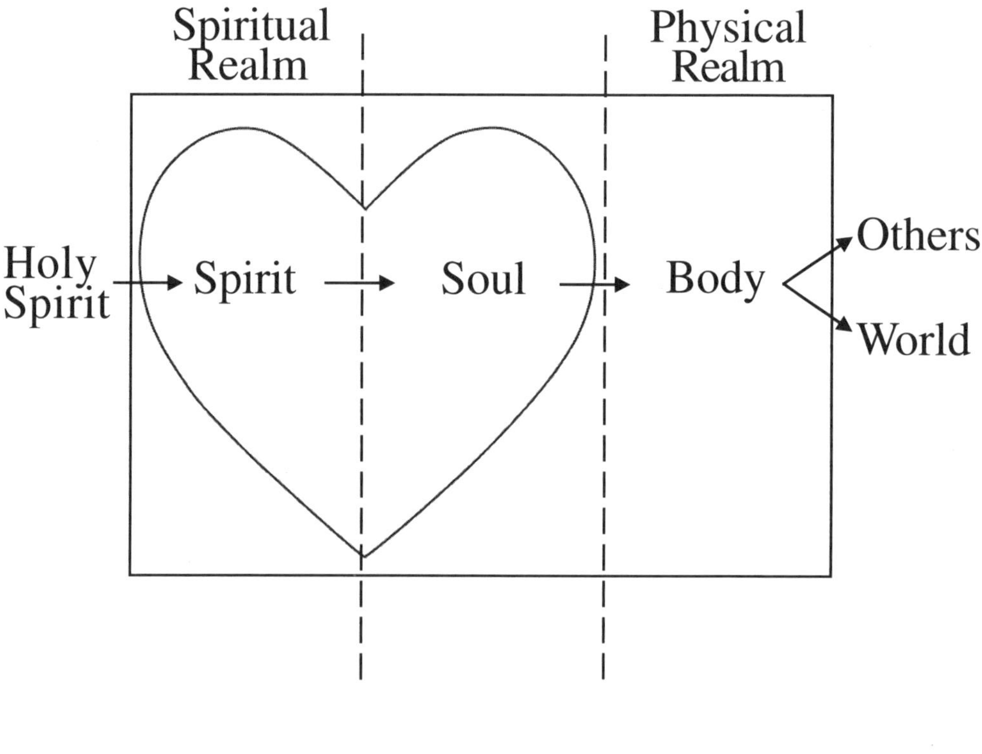

Part Four

The Fall

As the Holy Spirit continued to wash the lies and associated hurts from my deep mind and replace them with the truth of God's love for me, I came to see Scripture more clearly.

Before I had known little about what Satan had done to the human race through Adam's fall. I hadn't understood how he'd messed up the spirit, body and soul.

But now I began to see the extent of his evil schemes . . . and how they related to my issues.

CHAPTER 13

Broken Man

God created Adam and Eve and gave them the Garden of Eden in which to live. The garden was full of God. And in that place, in the cool of the day, God walked *with* the pair. God did not live *in* Adam and Eve, but they lived blanketed in His presence.

God caused two trees to grow in the center of that garden—the Tree of Life and the Tree of the Knowledge of Good and Evil. *And out of the ground the LORD God made every tree grow that is pleasant to the sight and good for food. The tree of life was also in the midst of the garden, and the tree of the knowledge of good and evil* (Genesis 2:9).

We were created to have a choice about our relationship with God; that choice was symbolized in the two trees. God did not arbitrarily make the fruit of the Forbidden Tree off limits to test the pair. The fruit of the Forbidden Tree was not good for man, so God tried to protect the first couple by warning them in strong terms not to eat it. He said, *Of every tree of the garden you may freely eat; but of the tree of the knowledge of good and evil you shall not eat, for in the day that you eat of it* ***you shall surely die*** (Genesis 2:16-17).

But the serpent came and deceived Eve.

> *Then the serpent said to the woman, **"You will not surely die.** For God knows that in the day you eat of it your eyes will be opened, and you will be like God, knowing good and evil." So when the woman saw that the tree was good for food, that it was pleasant to the eyes, and a tree desirable to make one wise, she took of its fruit and ate* (Genesis 3:4-6).

God created Adam in His image—to be like Him. But Adam and Eve opted to try and be "like God" apart from Him. That doesn't work. When the pair ate the Forbidden Fruit, they died by God's definition. By choosing to "be like God, knowing good and evil," they acted independently of God and separated themselves from His life-giving presence. Life apart from God is death by God's definition.

When Satan beguiled Eve, he had told her, "You will not surely die." And indeed, the pair did not die a physical death that day. The fruit did not contain a substance, like arsenic, that killed the body. The body could still move and eat, see and hear. Even though God's presence no longer blanketed and enlivened man, Adam and Eve appeared alive on the outside. This partial life was part of the cover-up Satan had crafted to make man think he was okay.

In pondering this, I came to realize that if God and Satan have different meanings of "death," they must also have different meanings of "life." I needed to know how God defined life and how Satan's definition differed from that. Satan disguises himself as an "angel of light" (see 2 Corinthians 11:14), so whatever the devil means by "life" has to look like life but not really be life at all.

The Greek uses two primary words for life—*psuche* and *zoe.* Life originating in the soul is termed *psuche* (which is the same word used for "soul"). *Psuche* is the life element of the soul. The life that we live on earth, including the visible physical life and the invisible life of the mind, will and emotions, is referred to as *psuche.* Thus, *psuche* life includes our moving limbs, beating heart and display of personality.

In the following Scriptures, the word "life" or "lives" is translated from the Greek *psuche: By this we know love, because He laid down His* ***life*** *for us. And we also ought to lay down our* ***lives*** *for the brethren* (1 John 3:16). *For whoever desires to save his* ***life*** *will lose it, but whoever loses his* ***life*** *for My sake will find it* (Matthew 16:25).

Zoe life, on the other hand, comes into our spirits when we accept Christ. It expresses the highest and best that Christ gives us. In God's design, *zoe* life is meant to fill our entire being. Jesus came to enliven the world with *zoe* life. We celebrate when a friend invites Jesus into his or her heart because a *zoe* life has begun.

In the following Scriptures, the word "life" is translated from the Greek *zoe: For God so loved the world that He gave His only begotten Son, that whoever believes in Him should not perish but have everlasting* ***life*** (John 3:16). *And this is eternal* ***life,*** *that they may know You, the only true God, and Jesus Christ whom You have sent* (John 17:3).

God intends for man to operate "in the Spirit" with *zoe* life flowing through the whole person of us. *Zoe* life is not meant to replace *psuche.* Rather, it is meant to meld and work in harmony with *psuche* to fill our whole being with eternal life. Scripture says, *The body without the spirit is dead* (James 2:26).

God elevates and perfects our whole being—spirit, soul and body—by letting *zoe* life flow through us so that we become the person we were meant to be. God did not come to kill off *psuche* life and smash our personality. Rather, He came to purify, refine and enliven the soul, thus making us our true selves. Our unique personalities come alive only in Him. God intends for His glory to radiate from our humanity.

But having been beguiled by Satan, Adam and Eve ate the fruit in a vain attempt to sustain *psuche* life apart from *zoe*. Now the soul had to govern itself with the "I will" of the individual. Mankind became autonomous—cut off from God. The closed system Adam and Eve had chosen for themselves didn't include God. Thus, man died by God's definition.

In this fallen state, the spirit was useless. It could no longer fulfill its purpose of communicating with God, guiding mankind and funneling *zoe* life to the soul and body parts. The pair had excluded God; there was no *zoe* life with which to connected.

This disconnection led to tragic breaks in relationship for Adam and Eve—and for all of us. The life of God could no longer flood through the watercourse of our humanity. The riverbed was dry. Lack of *zoe* life manifested itself in Broken Man—a man fractured into warring parts. Nothing works right without God.

The link between God and mankind is broken (see *a* in Figure 13). Scripture tells us, *And they heard the sound of the LORD God walking in the garden in the cool of the day, and Adam and his wife hid themselves from the presence of the LORD God* (Genesis 3:8).

The pair is uncomfortable with God's presence, so they hide. Now nothing of God's life can flow into the couple, and without *zoe* life, humanity can't function as designed. The bridge between the spiritual and physical realms has been rendered useless. Without *zoe* life flowing, every link in the human chain between God and the earth is nonfunctional. We are out of alignment with God, ourselves and the world.

The break of the soul-body connection (see *b* in Figure 13) is also clearly seen in Scripture. *Then the eyes of both of them were opened, and they knew that they were naked; and they sewed fig leaves together and made themselves coverings* (Genesis 3:7).

Upon eating the fruit, the two immediately felt they had to cover up their nakedness. With the soul in charge, the pair became susceptible to Satan's voice of accusation, and their newly "opened" eyes didn't like what they saw. The soul (mind) didn't like the body anymore; the two weren't in agreement. The soul, with its newfound knowledge of good and evil, wasn't satisfied with its outside covering. So the pair hid their bodies from themselves by covering up who they really were.

Thus, the God-intended alignment between soul and body was broken. There was a disconnect—a blocking of the watercourse—between the body and the soul.

But Satan was not done with his destruction of humanity. When questioned by God, Adam blamed Eve for the mess: *Then the man said, "The woman whom You gave to be with me, she gave me of the tree, and I ate"* (Genesis 3:12).

The "accuser of the brethren" (see Revelation 12:10) gets Adam to fault Eve. The man points the finger of blame at his wife. "She did it. It's because of her." People-to-people relationships are severed (see *c*).

The last and final relationship to be slashed is mentioned a bit later in Genesis 3. The ground is cursed. People will now have to survive by hard work (see Genesis 3:17-19). Without the flow of *zoe* life, the connection between man and the world is out of alignment (see *d*).

Thus, United Man—mankind united with God, aligned within himself and in connection with others and the world—is no more. Without God and the flow of *zoe* life—with the independent soul as ruler—none of the pieces fit properly with the others. United Man is now Broken Man. He is fragmented within himself and cut off from others.

The watercourse by which God designed that His light, life and love flow into and through man is dry. And that parched watercourse has been dammed up. It has been strewn with rocks and boulders so that even if water does once again enter the channel, it won't flow freely.

Satan's goal is Broken Man—a man separated into weak and warring factions. He is well aware that a kingdom or a house divided against itself cannot stand (see Mark 3:24-25). He knows that a branch severed from the vine—cut off from life-giving sap—bears no fruit (see John 15:4).

By getting the pair to eat the fruit, Satan had taken humans—the most treasured and loved of God's creatures—and broken them into pieces. He had messed up the only creatures designed to bridge the gap between the spiritual and earthly realms and convey God's blessings to the world. Satan knew that through mankind would come God's light, life and love to the earth, resulting in his demise, and so he tried to ensure that we would not fulfill our God-given destiny.

As a descendant of Adam, I, too, was broken into pieces. And because of these breaks, the *zoe* life of God wasn't filling my entire being. Indeed, I was born again; my spirit was alive. But the *zoe* life in my spirit wasn't flooding my soul and body. Rather than a river of God's love flowing through me, rocks and boulders littered the watercourse of my humanity so that only a slow drip, drip, drip leaked out.

And because I had been oblivious to this deception, I'd tried in my own strength—with the *psuche* life of my soul—to add to that meager flow. This I did, not by pressing into God for His *zoe* life to flood my complete being and wash out the debris, but by looking to myself to produce commendable deeds.

Indeed, from the outside, things appeared better when I did commendable works. By them I deceived myself and others into thinking I was actually full of God's *zoe* life and love. Thus, I became an expert at clothing my body in an external form of godliness that looked good but lacked the power of the real thing.

After eating of the Forbidden Tree, Adam and Eve used fig leaves to hide the shame of their nakedness and make themselves acceptable in their own eyes. And I, in essence, was doing the same thing.

FIGURE 13

BROKEN MAN

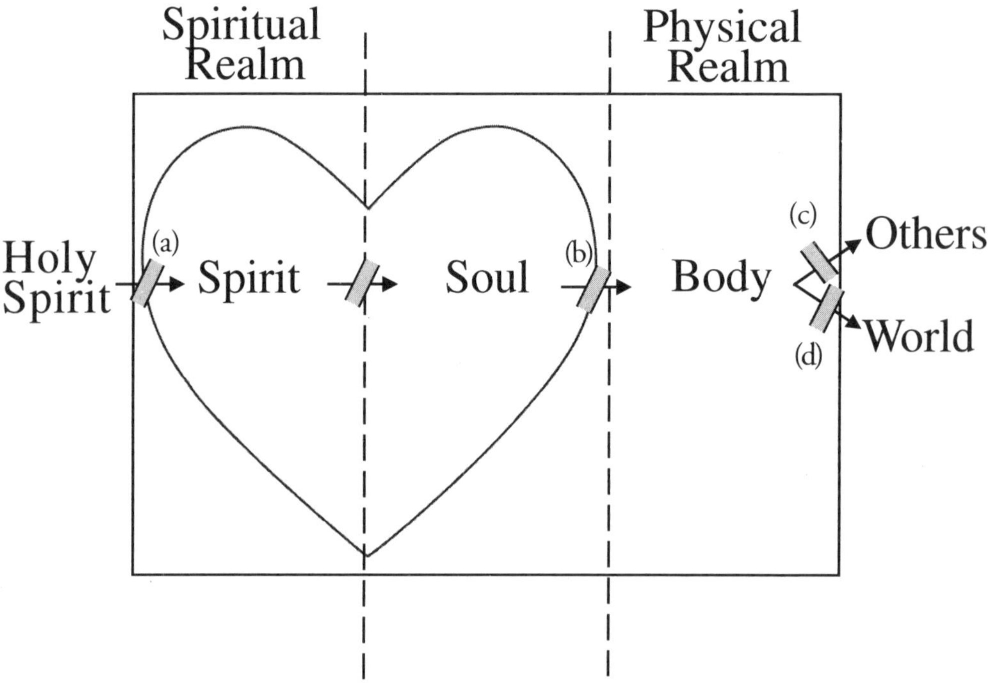

CHAPTER 14

Fig Leaves and Other Disguises

When God started showing me His way of love and the role of the soul in that, it didn't come in the logical story form written here. Rather, scattered bits and pieces began to take shape like parts of a jigsaw puzzle. One of the first parts I saw clearly were the fig leaves. Before I could let God make things right inside, I had to take off the disguise and realize who I really was.

Satan has been fooling man with fig leaves for a long time. He uses them to hide people from themselves. I had been so clothed in that façade myself that I couldn't see the disguise for what it was.

Once Adam and Eve ate the Forbidden Fruit and *zoe* life stopped flowing, the soul didn't like the body anymore. So the pair tried to cover up who they really were and make themselves presentable (to themselves and to their image of God) by clothing themselves with fig leaves. Scripture tells us, *Then the eyes of both of them were opened, and they knew that they were naked; and they sewed fig leaves together and made themselves coverings* (Genesis 3:7).

Adam with his newly "opened" eyes attempted to gain favor with God by making himself look acceptable on the surface. He dressed himself in his own efforts using coverings supplied by the world. Fig leaves make us think that we are presentable. Clothed in the disguise, we say to ourselves and others, "I am good."

Still today, regardless of age, culture or religious upbringing, we use external coverings to hide our sins and weaknesses. Rather than face the truth of who we really are, we put on "makeup" in order to look acceptable in our own eyes and in the eyes of God as we think He sees us. Our Adamic tendency is to try to fix problems in ourselves, others or society by patching them up from the outside. Thus, we try to correct societal evils, for example, by delivering food aid, putting criminals behind bars or adding more laws.

But makeup and fig leaves aren't inner rightness. In fact, they hinder purity within by causing us to believe we are okay and have no need of deep change.

For most of my life, I too have been caught in the age-old deception of the fig leaves—of trying to fix internal problems with polished-armor cover-ups. Let me give an example.

One Sunday morning soon after we moved to the Sacramento area, my turn came to watch the 3- and 4-year-olds during the second service at church. I should have said "no" and explained about my MS, but I thought it my responsibility as a good parent and Christian. So I pulled myself together and took my turn.

Anne, almost 4, was in the preschool room with me. One particular girl, by far the oldest in the class, took water from the sink and purposely poured it on the floor. I asked her to stop; she didn't. I took her aside and explained that I needed her cooperation so I could care for the younger children; that didn't help either. I put her in "time out"; she wouldn't stay in the chair. Finally, I told her, "If you don't stop acting like that, I am going to have to spank you."

I wouldn't have actually spanked a child who was not my own, but the threat worked. She quit misbehaving, and I was able to help the younger children.

But . . . she went home and told her parents what I had said. Her dad called me on the phone. He was not happy, and he was a lawyer.

I tried to explain the situation. He got more upset. In the heat of the discussion, I spurted out a lie. I told him I'd actually said to his daughter, "If you were my child and you acted like that, I would have to spank you." He accepted that, and our conversation ended peacefully.

But I had lied and that bothered me. Soon afterward, the little girl's mother, whom I had never met, became pregnant with their second child. I heard through the prayer chain that she had preeclampsia and needed bedrest. So I volunteered to take care of the girl after her preschool on Tuesdays and Thursdays. Twice a week for about five months, I, who could barely care for my own children, would drive across town, get her from school and drive back to our house, where she played with Anne until her father picked her up after work.

It wasn't until I began to understand about the fig leaves that God brought the whole thing back to my memory with vivid clarity. I realized I had given that free babysitting 15-plus years earlier, not out of love, but to cover up my lie and convince myself that I was indeed a good person.

What a lot of work to hide one lie! And I still felt guilty anyway. So I phoned the parents, whom I hadn't seen in years. They vaguely recalled the story. I told them the truth and asked them to forgive me. Then I no longer needed that fig leaf.

In my life, I have repeatedly done commendable deeds to hide my sin. And I have noticed that the greater the sin, the bigger and "better" the fig leaf needed to cover it.

But fig leaves are a primitive form of disguise; other cover-ups are much more sophisticated—like "whitewash." Jesus confronted the scribes and Pharisees: *You are like whitewashed tombs which indeed appear beautiful outwardly, but inside are full of dead men's bones and all uncleanness. Even so you also outwardly appear righteous to men, but inside you are full of hypocrisy and lawlessness* (Matthew 23:27-28).

The Pharisees made their outside behaviors—the actions of their bodies—look commendable. They put on external rules and regulations to make themselves appear acceptable. This whitewash blinded the Pharisees; pride deadened them to their desperate need of a better way. They looked so good on the outside that they deceived themselves into thinking they had life and love on the inside as well.

But in actuality, all they had was a form of godliness—the Law—which they obeyed with great outward show. The Ten Commandments give a description of how love acts. The Pharisees clothed themselves in that description without having the love inside. They wore the disguise of external conformity to the Law without having the internal relationship by which obedience springs forth as part of *zoe* life.

But Jesus wasn't fooled by the whitewash. He saw the "dead men's bones" within.

I once read a statement: *A cup of sweet tea, no matter how much it is jostled, spills nothing but sweet tea.*

How true! How simple! In the trials, testings and temptations of life—when we are jostled—what is really in us will come out. When our defenses are worn thin, the unspeakable will burst from our lips or slip from our hands. And the words or actions will surprise even us.

In my case, the temptation was a divorced man with a listening ear and a shoulder to cry on in the months surrounding my mother's death.

"Where did that come from?" I screamed at myself after the affair. If it had come out of me, it had to be in me. I agonized. I hung my head in shame. I condemned myself. . . .

And then I pulled myself together and put on more rules. I redoubled my "dedication" to Christ by asking God to help me be good and plastering on more commendable deeds while ignoring the root cause in my soul altogether. I imposed "Christlike" behaviors on my body in the hopes that it wouldn't manifest the contents of my contaminated soul (of which I was oblivious).

I sealed myself off with thicker, shinier armor—with more rules, greater self-condemnation and harsher punishments. I believed this would prevent whatever was inside from coming out. I didn't know any other way, and I couldn't afford to let that happen again.

After the affair, I became even more wary of sin. I made an unconscious vow that no sin would escape. I would not let one bit of my inner self show. No wonder I couldn't love; I was afraid to be anything but a shell of acceptable behaviors and words.

Looking back on it now, it is obvious why my husband, Dennis, went "looking for love in all the wrong places." Not much love was coming out of me. Fear of not being loved by God prevented me from letting Him in to deal with the root cause of the sin. In some distorted way I felt that if I let God see my impure inner self, He couldn't possibly love me. I couldn't believe God or anybody else loved me very much because I'd sinned and therefore didn't feel I deserved it. And because I couldn't really believe God loved me, I had little love to give away.

God didn't intend life to be this way. Jesus came to fix the sin problem from the inside. He wants to make the tea sweet. Then the more we are jostled, persecuted, hurt, maligned—even nailed to a cross—the more sweet tea will pour forth.

But there lurks yet another body covering more deceptive than fig leaves or whitewash—graveclothes. Those tight, white linen wrappings especially affect us Christians today.

The Bible tells us about Lazarus: *[Jesus] cried with a loud voice, "Lazarus, come forth!" And he who had died came out bound hand and foot with graveclothes, and his face was wrapped with a cloth. Jesus said to them, "Loose him, and let him go"* (John 11:43-44).

Lazarus is alive! God has done a miracle!

But the man is covered in graveclothes from head to foot. The wrappings imprison him like a giant cocoon. Graveclothes are the most restrictive and stifling of disguises. At least fig leaves and whitewash allow free movement. Lazarus is alive on the inside, but he is so horribly bound up on the outside that he looks dead.

In Lazarus' condition I saw myself. On the inside I was truly alive; I was saved in my spirit. But from the outside, I appeared dead. Layer upon layer of graveclothes had me bound so life and love couldn't flow.

Lazarus came back to life, but the graveclothes did not automatically fall off when he did. Rather, Jesus encouraged those gathered around, "Loose him, and let him go." Jesus specifically left to others the job of taking off the graveclothes.

God awakens the spirit, but He leaves to us the awesome responsibility and privilege of assisting in unbinding the person and setting them free. We get to help our brothers and sisters take off the outer coverings so that the light, life and love of Christ in them can radiate out in its fullness. God grants us the joy of assisting others in becoming free.

Something deep inside of me (and others I know) wants to be rid of graveclothes—open and honest before God and others. From earliest memory, I had desired something I didn't have words for at the time, but that I now know is to live life in the freedom of Christ. *Therefore if the Son makes you free, you shall be free indeed* (John 8:36).

Seeing the fig leaves, whitewash and graveclothes for what they really are has helped me greatly. With that shiny-armor façade stripped away, I came to more desperately desire inner rightness—God's real cure from the inside.

But before I could fully embrace the love of God and experience that inner purity, I had to understand what happened to our soul after Adam and Eve ate the Forbidden Fruit. In the Fall, Satan had deadened the spirit and stopped the flow of *zoe* life, thus breaking us into pieces. He had deglorified the body and deceived us into covering up our true condition.

And he had twisted our thinking by planting lies deep in the soul.

CHAPTER 15

Twisted Thinking

Satan is called "the father of lies." He is also called "the enemy of our souls"—not "the enemy of our spirits" nor "the enemy of our bodies," but "the enemy of our *souls.*" It was into the core of humanity—into the soul of Adam and Eve—that the devil infused his evil lies.

I had to understand what those lies were. In order to live and love as God intended, I needed to know how my own thoughts were similarly contaminated.

Satan's nature is one of pride. He is all about "I will." He is bent on making himself like God. Satan said, ***I will*** *ascend into heaven,* ***I will*** *exalt my throne above the stars of God;* ***I will*** *also sit on the mount of the congregation on the farthest sides of the north;* ***I will*** *ascend above the heights of the clouds,* ***I will be like the Most High*** (Isaiah 14:13-14).

And the devil tries to get us to fall in similar fashion—through tempting us to become like God by elevating the "I will" of ourselves. Through the fruit of the Forbidden Tree, Satan infused into the pair his pride-filled, "I will" nature and mindset.

The serpent came to Eve saying, *"For God knows that in the day you eat of it your eyes will be opened, and* ***you will be like God,*** *knowing good and evil." So when the woman saw that the tree was good for food, that it was pleasant to the eyes, and a tree desirable to make one wise, she took of its fruit and ate* (Genesis 3:5-6).

The deep deception was that the fruit would elevate her mind and enhance her soul life. Satan had promised, "Your eyes will be opened." "You will know good and evil." "You will be wise." "You will be like God."

Mankind was designed to be fully alive through spirit connection to God—through *zoe* life. But in the Fall, the God-given authority of the spirit was displaced, and we became beings ruled by the "I will" of ourselves. Now our Adamic predisposition is to function under the guidance of our autonomous souls, not under God's leading as directed through our spirits.

After eating the fruit, the pair believed the lie that they could become good—like God—apart from Him. Because they were wise and knew the difference between good and evil, the twisted belief was that they could now become good by doing good things. The puffed-up soul thought it could become like God by acting commendably.

What deception. What pride. No good exists apart from God. He is the source of all good.

But Adam and Eve had chosen an autonomous life apart from God. So rather than being raised up to the good of God by God Himself, we became puffed up—like Satan had puffed himself up—by thinking we could become good on our own. *Knowledge puffs up, but love edifies* (1 Corinthians 8:1). Rather than humble beings led by God through our spirits, we humans became prideful beings led by our souls. The elevated soul thus usurped the position God had designed for the spirit through which the life of God could energize the creature. We were in charge of ourselves.

The Forbidden Fruit soiled Adam's mind in another way as well; fear now filled his soul. After eating of the fruit, Adam said to God, *I heard Your voice in the garden, and I was* ***afraid*** *because I was naked; and I hid myself* (Genesis 3:10). This is the first time the word "afraid" is used in the Bible.

But why is Adam afraid? God has never done anything but give him a luscious garden full of food to eat and animals to name. God has given him a beautiful wife too, and He walks with them in the cool of the garden. Why would Adam suddenly be afraid?

The knowledge of good and evil makes Adam afraid of not measuring up by definition of his newly gained wisdom. He feels he has to be good, so that he can be like God. And when he does wrong, he fears the punishment he believes God will inflict upon him.

Before eating the Forbidden Fruit, Adam knew God's love and goodness as something as right and natural as air. But now Adam's mind (soul) is contaminated and distracted. No longer is life effortless and free in the loving care of God. Instead, his focus has shifted; his thoughts are consumed with self. What must he do to be acceptable to God? How will he muster good and avoid evil?

It is as if Adam has put on mirrored glasses that focus his vision inward. All of life now is seen through the distorted lenses tainted by his puffed-up view of self and the fear of God. Man must try his hardest to avoid evil things and do good deeds so as to dodge the wrath of God.

For Adam, life became one of *fear-based doing* rather than one of *love-based being. Fear-based performance,* rather than *love-based relationship,* now define man's existence.

The Tree of the Knowledge of Good and Evil has distorted Adam's perception. He sees God through his own newly "opened" eyes as a God who judges on a good/evil scale and punishes imperfection. Adam views

God as a demanding judge waiting for a slipup so He can condemn him to death. This is how "the father of lies" would have us think of God.

And Adam's perception of the good he believes God requires is twisted in definition. "Good" to Adam and Eve is a construct defined by the Tree of the Knowledge of Good and Evil. It is something in the closed system of man apart from God that looks commendable on the surface. "Good" looks deceptively like what God would do, but isn't done in unity with Him.

For a person thinking with a Forbidden Tree mindset, Satan works his evil schemes either as "the accuser of the brethren" for those who feel they have done evil or disguised as "an angel of light" for those who feel they have done good. It doesn't matter to him which deception holds his prisoners captive. Both spell eternal death.

Under the Tree of the Knowledge of Good and Evil, "good" is represented by the Pharisee, while "evil" is represented by the tax collector or the woman caught in adultery. Neither is living life as God intends, but the tax collector and adulterer at least understand their sinful condition. The prideful Pharisee does not. The good—the whitewash—has blinded his eyes so that he actually thinks of himself as a good person. In a Forbidden Tree mindset, good is much more deceptive than evil.

The vast majority of humanity (even redeemed humanity) is caught in this struggle of trying to do good things to earn God's favor and love. Most of us seek to be obedient and do commendable things under the system of our unique beliefs and values. Buddhists may try to be obedient by emptying themselves so as to attain a state of nirvana in which one has no feelings, desires or wants at all. Radical Muslims may believe that ultimate good is martyring oneself for the cause of Allah. A few years ago, I read about a holy Hindu man who, because of his definition of "good," crawled on his belly more than 125 kilometers to the top of a holy mountain in India where he stabbed his only son to death.

These good behaviors sound ridiculous to most Americans. Depending on our exact mindset, good to us is likely to be defined by some jumbled conglomeration of Wall Street, Hollywood and Harvard. But regardless of whether we see it or not, we in the United States are also stuck in the mindset of trying to do commendable deeds as defined by our culture.

As Christians, we hold a yet different definition of "good"—a strongly biblical definition. We do good by building homes for the poor, providing food to the hungry, sharing the Good News with others, praying for people and so on. Indeed, Jesus encouraged us to do these types of things. But Christianity is not about right definitions of good behaviors. It has nothing to do with trying to follow a set of guidelines—despite the fact that those guidelines may have biblical roots. True Christianity is not about focussing our attention on staying within the boundaries outlined by a good set of external rules; it is about staying in love relationship with God.

The New Testament was not written to provide a revised set of higher-standard rules with Jesus added to give us the strength to meet the updated requirements. The New Covenant is not a law-based system. It is grace based and comes with a whole new way of thinking and being. Jesus ushered in an entirely new way. Under the New Covenant, good is not defined in terms of *doing* things; it is defined in terms of *being* in relationship.

Good flows from God—from the Holy Spirit, in connection with our spirit, in connection with our soul. Commendable, on the other hand, flow from an autonomous soul cut off from life-giving connection.

God does not want us to do anything apart from Him—no matter how pretty it looks. Jesus warns that many (who probably would call themselves "Christians") will be deceived on this account. *Many will say to Me in that day, "Lord, Lord, have we not prophesied in Your name, cast out demons in Your name, and done many wonders in Your name?" And then I will declare to them, "I never knew you; depart from Me, you who practice lawlessness!"* (Matthew 7:22-23).

We cannot please God apart from relationship with Him; in relationship with God, we always please Him. God wants us to let His light, life and love flow through the watercourse of our being like sap flows from the vine to the branches. John 15:4 says, *Abide in Me, and I in you. As the branch cannot bear fruit of itself, unless it abides in the vine, neither can you, unless you abide in Me.*

But I had not seen this clearly. If I did commendable deeds, I believed I was good and right with God. Adam's twisted mindset had warped my thoughts. I'd believed the lie that if you do commendable things, God will love you, but if you don't, He won't.

That lie had warped the framework of my life in several ways. First, I tried desperately to do commendable things. In high school I got straight As. I played number one on the tennis team. I was president of the Girl's League and of the California Scholarship Federation. I was prom queen. At Stanford the trend continued: two separate degrees in four years, an amazing GPA, graduating with honors and distinction. Graduate school. Numerous publications. Helping starving children in Kenya. Raising four kids. Working for a mission organization. Nothing was enough. Life was a constant struggle to accomplish the impossible and be good . . . so that I could earn love from others and God.

As a second related characteristic of my life, I lived in fear of evil. I knew Jesus had erased my past sins, but the sins I might commit tomorrow, what about those? Would He still love me if I didn't obey?

I was so afraid of evil bursting forth that I put all sorts of external rules on myself to make my behavior conform to my highly religious definition of "good." I dressed myself nicely, smiled and went to church. Then I came home, read my Bible and listened to praise music.

Interacting with the real world scared me because I might get jostled so that sin broke out. I was stiff and hard, especially after the affair. My behavior was proper and controlled; I couldn't afford to let that happen again.

Rather than being free to do things out of love, I was motivated by fear—fear of either not doing enough commendable things to deserve love or fear of doing evil and therefore being disqualified to receive love. Thus, I acted to earn love, not as a consequence of being loved. Fear, not love, underlay the motivation for what I did . . . and for the person I was.

Life was a series of commendable deeds to cross off my nice, neat, to-do list for the day. Getting the job done "right" drove me. I was a human *doing,* not a human *being.*

But love doesn't flow from human *doings.* Love isn't something that can be checked off a to-do list.

A third major characteristic of my life under the foundational lie was that I constantly judged myself. "Was I measuring up? How could I be more efficient so I could cram more good into the day?" I was rushed and hurried trying to do more commendable things.

For everything I did, I mentally gave myself either a black mark or a gold star. The black marks made me feel guilty, ashamed and condemned. The gold stars fed my pride. It was a lose/lose situation with no solution . . . under that system of unrenewed thinking.

And I judged friends, relatives, my husband and children too with the same yardstick I used to evaluate myself.

Imagine having a father like that . . . or a mother.

Without realizing what I was doing, I pressured Jake, Bryn, Anne and Mark to do commendable things, tried to get them to keep away from evil . . . and unknowingly withheld my love from them if they didn't meet these expectations.

And I was doing all this with Christ in my spirit, but not in the essence of my being—in my soul. I had a New Covenant spirit, but I wasn't thinking with a New Covenant mind. Scripture says, *For as [a man] thinks in his heart, so is he* (Proverbs 23:7). But I wasn't thinking as God intended—with the "mind of Christ" (see 1 Corinthians 2:16).

Instead of radiating love, I was spewing out judgment cloaked in a shiny-armor façade of commendable deeds. This is what Edna had referred to that day; others felt—instead of love—a rushed, plastic, aloof perfection tainted with alternating condemnation or pride. Imagine broadcasting that version of "Christianity" to the world.

Needless to say, I didn't see any of this at the time. I was a "strong Christian" by church standards. The lie passed down from the Forbidden Tree went much deeper than conscious awareness and colored even my interpretation of Scripture. Thus, the lie itself dammed up the truth needed to wash it away.

I don't want my old ways of thought to limit God. I want to see God as He really is and I want to be the creature He created me to be. Scripture says, *When He is revealed, we shall be like Him, for we shall see Him as He is* (1 John 3:2). I had to know the real Jesus and let His Words define me as a human being. I knew God had a way for me to live and love as He intended.

And I saw His master plan more and more clearly as the lies continued to fall away.

Part Five

Restoration: God's Done Deal

After the Fall, God began the gradual process of restoring us humans. Through the Old Covenant, we learned that knowledge about good and evil wasn't enough to make us the people God intended.

Then Jesus came as the Son of Man to fix the problem the only way it could really be fixed—from the inside. Through the cross, He fulfilled the Old Covenant and made a completely New Covenant.

And all God's dealings with us were grounded in His love.

CHAPTER 16

The Way Back

Despite Adam and Eve's rebellion, God loved the pair—and their descendants. He had fashioned us humans in His image; He would not give up on us.

Once Adam and Eve ate the Forbidden Fruit, God began the gradual work of restoring mankind to his pre-fallen state . . . and to an even more glorious existence. With lovingkindness He drew mankind back to Himself so that we could know His love in personal relationship. *His lovingkindness is everlasting* (1 Chronicles 17:34, NASB).

As a first step in the restoration process, God had to make it clear to us humans that we needed Him—that we were not created to be governed by our own independent souls. Satan had tricked Adam and Eve into eating the Forbidden Fruit by telling them, "You will be like God, knowing good and evil." Now God had to help humanity realize that trying to be like God in this fashion—with the soul and its knowledge of good and evil leading the way—couldn't make us right.

Before God could restore humanity to its original formation, we first had to acknowledge that we could never be like God through the means

Satan had promised. We had to learn for ourselves that autonomy in a system without God—the Forbidden Tree system—didn't work. God brought this realization through the Old Covenant.

The rules of the Old Covenant—the Ten Commandments—were inscribed on stone tablets, and Moses carried them down the mountain to the people. Adam and Eve had excluded God from direct relationship with the human race, so God had to help from outside the system by defining "good" and "evil" in clear terms. The Ten Commandments were His way of doing that.

The Law came from the outside, and people had to work themselves up to obedience. They had to try their hardest on their own—with the strength of the autonomous soul separated from the *zoe* life of God.

The rules were that if man obeyed the Ten Commandments God would prosper him. People were to fulfill their half of the Old Covenant by following the guidelines God had set forth. The Ten Commandments told people what they must *do* and what they must *not do* to receive God's favor. Blessings came with obeying the Law; curses came with disobedience.

Over and over, God reiterated this principle throughout the Old Testament. *Obey My voice, and I will be your God, and you shall be My people. And walk in all the ways that I have commanded you, that it may be well with you* (Jeremiah 7:23). *Cursed is the man who does not obey the words of this covenant* (Jeremiah 11:3).

This is the way things worked under the system defined by the Tree of the Knowledge of Good and Evil. Adam and Eve had selected for themselves a system that excluded God. God was outside the system looking in, but He was not within the system itself. He loved man, but He couldn't love him up close and personal because Adam and Eve had chosen to step out of relationship and live independently, guided by the leading of the soul with its knowledge of good and evil.

Under the Old Covenant, God could only encourage people by showing them the need to reestablish relationship. He did this by giving sound rules about what was good and what was evil . . . and then letting man learn through his repeated failure that this was not enough. God gave guidance through the Old Covenant to show that knowledge about good and evil wasn't sufficient; it didn't give people the strength to consistently choose the good. It didn't bring them into relationship with God whereby good flowed from the Source within.

Under the Old Covenant, it was man's job to try to love. In fact, the most important commandments under the Old Covenant were about love. People were to love God with all the strength they could muster on their own. And they were to love their neighbors like they loved themselves.

I had tried to do that too. Although I was saved, in some distorted way I was still living under the Old Covenant and trying to generate the good works and the love myself. I believed in Jesus, but I didn't know enough to believe in His complete, finished work.

But the Old Covenant didn't work for the Hebrews . . . and it didn't work for me. We humans fail miserably at keeping the Ten Commandments, at loving in our own strength and at loving others like we love ourselves. As Jesus told the disciples, *With men this is impossible* (Matthew 19:26); we weren't meant to live by obedience to some set of external guidelines. *But with God all things are possible;* we were meant to live in love relationship with God.

God wanted to bless the Hebrews, but He was limited in doing so. The Old Covenant had conditions, and people couldn't fulfill their half of the bargain. Under the Law, blessings are conditional, but we humans can't meet those conditions. Therefore, as I had personally experienced, attaining God's favor through obedience to some set of good rules is impossible.

Even God's chosen failed miserably at keeping the Old Covenant. Look at the early kings, for example. The first king, Saul, was plagued with horrible jealousies and tried repeatedly to have David killed. The next king, David, "a man after God's own heart" (see 1 Samuel 13:14), had an affair and then killed the unsuspecting husband. Then Solomon, the wisest of all, took foreign wives in abundance and brought their false gods into his kingdom.

The Law, which defined "good" and "evil" in detail, was not sufficient to produce good people. It defined the good, but it did not provide the means for us to become good. It told us to love God and our neighbors, but it did not supply the love to be given away. All the laws and commandments given from the outside can't make us right, because we are not right apart from God.

Even so, the Law served its purpose. It showed us our utter sinfulness and inability apart from life-giving connection with God. The Law was the schoolmaster of our outer man designed to teach us of our desperate need to be free of sin in the inner man. The Old Covenant was given to show us our self-*in*sufficiency—to drive us to God for the life available to us only in Christ Jesus.

Because they didn't have God inside, people living in Old Testament times relied on His transient, external anointing. Without it, they were helpless. Saul, for example, was fearful, but when the Spirit of God came upon him, he prophesied mightily (see 1 Samuel 10:10). Samson was weak when the Spirit departed from him (see Judges 16:20). For this reason, David knew to plead: *Do not cast me away from Your presence, and do not take Your Holy Spirit from me* (Psalm 51:11).

Deep within himself, Old Testament man knew things weren't right. The Old Testament prophets and patriarchs longed for a right spirit. Job cried, *My spirit is broken* (Job 17:1). David prayed, *Renew a steadfast spirit within me* (Psalm 51:10). These cries expressed man's desperate need for drastic change. Old Testament people realized that their only hope lay in the promise of a whole new way.

And that better way came, not from God's external anointing from the outside, but from God taking up residence inside. Long before Christ appeared, the prophets had foretold of this new way: *I will give you a new heart and put a new spirit within you; I will take the heart of stone out of your flesh and give you a heart of flesh. I will put My Spirit within you* (Ezekiel 36:26-27).

The New Covenant was strikingly different from the Old. It was written on human hearts. God came to dwell within—in our spirit.

As a human being, Jesus restored all that Adam lost in the Fall. He did for us what we could not do for ourselves. By choosing to let God direct all He was and did, by surrendering His will and choosing to be led by the Spirit, Jesus met the requirements of the Old Covenant and established a New Covenant. In the New Covenant, God does our part for us; our only requirement is to enter by faith into His finished work and live in love relationship with Him.

The One Command under the New Covenant—to love one another as He loved us—does not abolish the Ten Commandments; it fulfills them. Jesus said, *Do not think that I came to destroy the Law or the Prophets. I did not come to destroy but to fulfill* (Matthew 5:17). The Law of Christ—the Law of Love—brings to living fullness the Law of Moses. Romans 13:10 tells us, *Love does no harm to a neighbor; therefore love is the fulfillment of the law.*

But in my warped thinking, I somehow believed that with Jesus in me—with His help—I was to fulfill the rules and regulations of the Old Covenant. I thought that, with Him, I was supposed to be able to do what the Old Testament kings could not and obey the Ten Commandments. So I kept looking back to the old Law to see if I were measuring up . . . but I wasn't.

Even with a new spirit within me I didn't measure up . . . because Jesus hadn't come to enable me to reach that mark. Rather, He came to give me Himself and elevate me out of the old system entirely. On the cross, He fulfilled the Old Covenant for me so I no longer needed to measure myself by the old standard. I didn't need to keep looking back at it.

What does it mean to "fulfill" a requirement? When I fulfilled the requirements for my bachelor's degree, those requirements still existed, but I no longer had to live by them. They were not abolished, but they were fulfilled. Now I was free to move on and work toward my Ph.D. The old still existed, but it was fulfilled. I had that degree. Now I could move on to the new.

So it is with the Old and New Covenants. Jesus fulfilled the Old totally and completely. He did not come to enable us, with His help, to fulfill the Old. Rather, He did it all for us. Under the New Covenant, the Old Covenant laws are fulfilled, not by looking back at them, but by looking forward to Christ Jesus. With Him, we live in the freedom of the New.

Under the New Covenant, it isn't up to us to try to obey, generate good works or love like I was attempting to do. Under the New, God supplies the love that makes us able to love others. Under the New, it isn't about us humans loving Him in all our strength or loving our neighbors like we love ourselves. It's not about *us* at all. It's about loving people with the love He gives us to share.

In the New Covenant, God supplies everything. We can't break the New Covenant because all its conditions have been met. The price has been paid in full. God did our part for us because He knew we could never do it ourselves.

Our only requirement in the New Covenant is to believe. By believing, we enter into His finished work and let His love pour through us. It is a love covenant. The price to partake of the eternal blessings have been paid for by His blood. All we need to do is believe that God wants us to be in love relationship with Him and that He has made a way for that to happen. In relationship, all the promises of the New Covenant are ours by inheritance.

The New Covenant comes with a totally fresh way of thinking and living. Nothing need be earned; nothing can be earned. In the New Covenant, everything of *zoe* life—of God's light, life and love—is given as a free gift.

God desires that I stay in life-giving, love relationship with Him. The gift comes through relationship. He wants me to believe in His love so that what He has already given can become mine. He doesn't want me looking back at the Old Covenant with all its rules and regulations and working hard to keep from failing by Old Covenant standards. I am not under the Old. I am living in the freedom of the New.

Jesus came as the last Adam to give us a fresh start. And He modeled that new way of living for us in His humble life on earth as the Son of Man.

CHAPTER 17

Jesus, Son of Man

As I began to understand, Jesus came as a human being to show us the truth of how God made us to be fully human beings ourselves. As a man, Jesus modeled life the way we were created to live it.

God wouldn't have been able to demonstrate complete humanness for us unless He had become human Himself. Jesus walked this earth as a man. He remained God—100 percent God—but He voluntarily laid aside all use of His divinity when He came to earth.

In this sense, Jesus was like us. He was tempted and tried in all things (see Hebrews 4:15) and was not given an extra amount of grace, strength or power to overcome Satan's attacks. Rather, He humbled Himself and depended (like we are designed to) on the Holy Spirit to accomplish God's will through Him.

Jesus' favorite name for Himself is the "Son of Man." For example, in the book of Matthew, Jesus refers to Himself 35 times. Thirty of these times, He calls Himself the "Son of Man." In the book of Mark, He refers to Himself 15 times—14 times as the "Son of Man." Others, such as the disciples, those He healed and Satan, refer to Him as the "Son of

God" or the "Son of David," but Jesus repeatedly calls Himself the "Son of Man."

As a man, Jesus accomplished His mission and wielded power and authority on earth. He fulfilled the Old Covenant requirements and established the New *as a man.*

It had to be this way because God designed that He would replenish and rule the earth through human beings. The title "man" carries with it all God's promised blessing for the earth. Back in Genesis, God had told Adam, *Fill the earth and subdue it; have dominion over the fish of the sea, over the birds of the air, and over every living thing that moves on the earth* (Genesis 1:28). God gave us humans authority to fill and subdue the earth.

Hebrews 2:6-8 says, *What is man that You are mindful of him? . . . You have crowned him with glory and honor, and set him over the works of Your hands. You have put all things in subjection under his feet.* God purposed to bless the earth, not through nature, not through animals, not through angels, but through us humans.

For this reason, it was essential that *as a man* Jesus accomplish everything necessary to restore us to our pre-fallen state of ruling and reigning. Thus, Jesus made a way and also modeled that way for us. The life He lived demonstrated how we are to operate in order to fulfill our destiny as members of the human race.

Everything Jesus spoke or did came from God. He said, *For the Father loves the Son, and shows Him all things that He Himself does* (John 5:20). In this way, Jesus was an unbroken watercourse. God came into Him and poured out through Him with nothing of the puffed-up, soul-independent, Adamic nature to obstruct the flow. By the complete surrender of His will, Jesus was filled with everything of God and lived in unbroken relationship with His Father.

Because of this, *through* Jesus, God reached down and touched the world with His love in a form we could relate to. *For God so loved the world that He gave His only begotten Son, that whoever believes in Him should not perish but have everlasting life. For God did not send His Son into the world to condemn the world, but that the world* ***through*** *Him might be saved* (John 3:16-17).

God touched the world *through* the surrendered humanity of His Son. Jesus as a man was a perfect unclogged watercourse *through* which God's love flowed. The teachings, the miracles, eternal life and love did not come *from* Jesus; they poured *through* Him. They came from God, passed *through* the Son of Man as a pure, clean channel and poured out to the world.

Nothing, absolutely nothing, came *from* Jesus Himself; it all came *through* Him as the Son of Man. Scripture repeats this for us over and over again: *All things were made* ***through*** *Him* (John 1:3); . . . *that all* ***through*** *Him might believe* (John 1:7); . . . *miracles, wonders, and signs which God did* ***through*** *Him in your midst* (Acts 2:22); . . . *and one Lord Jesus Christ,* ***through*** *whom are all things, and* ***through*** *whom we live* (1 Corinthians 8:6).

At every point in His life, Jesus' soul bent its knee to the Holy Spirit's leading as He knew it in His spirit. He never opted for His own will—His own, independent, soulical way. Jesus humbled Himself, allowing God through His spirit to govern His soul. Complete surrender to the Father's will characterized His life. Over and over again, He chose God's will in His soul. He said, *For I have come down from heaven,* ***not to do My own will, but the will of Him who sent Me*** (John 6:38).

Satan had said, ***I will*** *ascend into heaven,* ***I will*** *exalt my throne above the stars of God;* ***I will . . . I will . . . I will . . .*** (see Isaiah 14:13-14). And he had infused his pride-filled mindset into man. But Jesus came to break that way of thinking and living and to make us a new creation—filled and energized with the *zoe* life of God flowing into our humble humanity. Philippians 2:5-8 says, *Let this* ***mind*** *be in you which was also in Christ Jesus, who, being in the form of God, . . . made Himself of no reputation, taking the form of a bondservant, . . .* ***He humbled Himself*** *and became obedient to the point of death.*

Throughout His life, Jesus' strength—His life-giving food—came from continually embracing the will of God. Everything Jesus did and spoke came to Him from His spirit-to-Spirit connection with the Father. Doing the Father's will was His energy supply—the stuff that sustained Him. He said, *My food is to do the* ***will*** *of Him who sent Me, and to finish His work* (John 4:34).

The ultimate proof of Jesus' embracing of the Father's will came in the Garden of Gethsemane. Up to that point in His life, Jesus had been perfectly obedient. He had stayed in the love of God. His soul had relinquished its way to the Spirit in complete humility.

Now comes the final exam. All of hell comes against Jesus to pull Him from His purpose of being the last Adam and restoring man to his full created purpose. Except for His heavenly Father, He is alone; none of His closest friends stand with Him in the fight. In the dark of night He struggles. He falls on His face. His sweat becomes like drops of blood.

The Gospels of Matthew, Mark and Luke all share the story. Matthew 26:37-44 records it thus:

> *And He took with Him Peter and the two sons of Zebedee, and He began to be sorrowful and deeply distressed. Then He said to them, "****My soul is exceedingly sorrowful,*** *even to death. Stay here and watch with Me." He went a little farther and fell on His face, and prayed, saying, "O My Father, if it is possible, let this cup pass from Me; nevertheless,* ***not as I will, but as You will.****" . . . Again, a second*

> *time, He went away and prayed, saying, "O My Father, if this cup cannot pass away from Me unless I drink it,* ***Your will be done.****" And He . . . prayed the third time, saying the same words.*

Jesus' soul is in agony. The Father is asking from Him every bit of *psuche* life—every iota of "I will." This is contrary to the human nature of Jesus' soul. The "I" of Jesus—who He is in the core of His humanity—does not want to die. His soul is "exceedingly sorrowful."

But Jesus chooses what He knows in His spirit is God's will. He prays that His will—the will of His soul—be conformed to the will of His Father.

The watercourse remains unbroken. Jesus' soul holds steadfast in perfect alignment with God. In complete humility, He once again surrenders His desires and bends His soul to the leading of His Father as He knows it in His spirit.

Jesus takes the will of God into Himself and owns it as His. As He has done throughout His life, He casts aside the will of the "I" and receives God's will in replacement. By choosing to accept His Father's life and love, Jesus as a man is continuing to define Himself only by God. Thus, He again allows His Father's life and love to express itself in human form through Him.

By dawn of first light, everything in Jesus has been tested and found perfect. Tried in every respect, He is now ready to become the perfect sacrifice slain from the foundation of the world. His soul—His personality, the essence of Himself—is pure to the last drop. Jesus belongs only to God.

As the last Adam, Jesus has shown Himself to be as God originally designed Adam to be. He has become a man ruled by His spirit in perfect agreement and oneness with the Holy Spirit. Jesus has humbled Himself to the Spirit's leading. Father and Son are in perfect unity.

Jesus' will and the Father's are one and the same. Heaven and earth meet in the soul of Jesus. God's kingdom has come; God's will has been done on earth as it is in heaven. The Father has perfect expression in the Son. Jesus said, *He who has seen Me has seen the Father* (John 14:9).

With boldness, Jesus now moves forward. He tells His disciples, *The hour has come; behold, the Son of Man is being betrayed into the hands of sinners. Rise, let us be going* (Mark 14:41-42). With unshakable resolve, He now proceeds as He has always proceeded before—in the will and flow of His Father.

The Holy Spirit propels Him. He arises from prayer and meets the opposition head-on. To present His body is not the battle; the flesh-and-blood sacrifice of His body follows naturally from the leading of His soul in perfect unity with His Father.

He is taken before Pilate and questioned. His body is beaten and spit upon. A crown of thorns is pressed upon His head. Insults and mocking are hurled at Him. He is nailed to the cross.

Jesus said, *Greater love has no one than this, than to lay down one's life for his friends* (John 15:13). On the cross, Jesus demonstrated that "greater love." In all the galaxies, across all the epochs of time, in heaven itself, there is no greater love.

Just as a cup of sweet tea, no matter how much it is jostled, spills nothing but sweet tea, Jesus, jostled and shattered unto death, spilt nothing but pure, perfect love. Only love pours forth because nothing but God fills His soul. His will is God's. His soul is God's. He is God's. He is God.

In taking God's will—in staying united with the Father and opting not to act autonomously as the "I" of Himself would have chosen—Jesus fulfilled the Old Covenant and established the New. *[When] He said, "Behold, I have come to do Your **will,** O God," He takes away the first that He may establish the* *second. By that **will** we have been sanctified through the offering of the body of Jesus Christ* (Hebrews 10:9-10).

In the Garden of Eden, Adam had chosen death for the human race by eating of the Tree of the Knowledge of Good and Evil. By this choice, the human soul had become puffed up and mankind had become autonomous—separated from God.

But in the Garden of Gethsemane, Jesus chose *zoe* life for the human race by eating of the Tree of Life. By choosing God's will as His food, Jesus' soul bent its knee to the Spirit. Thus, the human spirit regained its right to life *and* its right to its God-given position of leadership.

By the complete surrender of His will—the dethroning of His soul—Jesus, the last Adam, became a "life-giving spirit." Scripture tells us, *The first man, Adam, became a living soul. The last Adam became a life-giving spirit* (1 Corinthians 15:45, NASB). Jesus lived His life on earth via His spirit-to-Spirit connection with the Father, not by the leading of His autonomous soul.

Praise God! In the Garden of Gethsemane, Jesus fully regained what Adam lost in the Garden of Eden. Now we can live with everything of God—His light, life and love, His total will—flowing to us, through us and out to the world. Through Jesus, Broken Man can become United Man. The spirit, soul and body, not just the spirit, can come alive with *zoe* life.

Upon Jesus' death, God ripped the veil in the temple separating the Holy of Holies from the inner court. The temple is no longer divided by a curtain that walls off the God-containing part from the other parts. No separation exists between God's dwelling place in the spirit (represented by the Holy of Holies) and the soul and body (represented by the inner and outer courts). God has access to the whole creature!

Jesus' life on earth serves as a model for our own. We humans are meant to be as Jesus was! Our Savior became "the firstborn among many brethren" (see Romans 8:29). God wants us to follow in the footsteps of His Son and let our Holy Spirit-filled spirit guide our soul. He "predestined us to adoption as sons" (see Ephesians 1:5).

But something major was wrong. When I took this understanding about Jesus' total obedience and submission to God and tried to make it work for me, it didn't. I couldn't consistently humble myself and obey like Jesus had. Sometimes I could surrender my will, but other times I couldn't.

So I tried harder. But I couldn't force my will to conform to the Holy Spirit's leading.

Looking back on it now, I see that I couldn't abide in the Father like Jesus had because He knew and believed, in the core of Himself, a monumentally important truth to which I was oblivious.

CHAPTER 18

The Father's Lavish Love

Questions whirled in my mind. What gave Jesus the ability as a man to choose to do only what He saw the Father doing? What gave Him the strength to speak only what He heard the Father speak? What enabled Jesus to stay in perfect unity with God and be a channel of the Father's light, life and love?

In my thinking, I had always answered those questions with the word "obedience." I believed that Jesus stayed tapped into the Father because He was obedient. I believed Jesus' surrender and sinlessness allowed Him to stay united with God. In my mind, Christ's obedience earned Him God's favor and love and allowed the unity whereby Jesus worked the works of God.

In that vein of thinking, I assumed that if I could just be obedient—just be good enough to earn His favor—then God would love me and I could stay in unity with Him. So I tried to be obedient. I tried with all my strength to be good and not sin.

Struggling to be good exhausted me; fear of being bad haunted me. In fact, good versus evil—determining which was which, trying to do the good and avoid the evil and attempting to help others do the same—occupied my thoughts and colored my behaviors. I spent more time thinking about these things (and acting on those thoughts) than I did enjoying God and the life He had given me.

Day after day, year after year, long after the affair was over (and long before it had begun), this endless cycle played in my life. When I judged myself to have sinned, for example by saying something I shouldn't have, ignoring one of the kids while trying to complete a project, having prideful thoughts and so on, either I would try harder not to sin by putting more external rules on myself, or I would try to hide my sin by dressing myself in an extra show of good behaviors.

Regardless of which tactic I used, I would condemn myself and feel guilty. Then I would ask God for forgiveness, vow to myself to do better tomorrow and seek Him for strength to go on.

Why couldn't I consistently obey? Why couldn't I walk in dependence upon God? I could be good for short periods, and when I was, I felt strong. But when I fell out of obedience, I felt disconnected from God and unworthy to claim the promises of Scripture. It was an endless cycle. I was not making progress in my self-conceived, religious rat race.

I would see a Scripture and try to hold onto it as the key to the promises that I knew were for me. For example, I saw the glorious promise in John 15:7: *If you abide in Me, and My words abide in you, you will ask what you desire, and it shall be done for you.* But I felt I couldn't abide, because abiding required obedience, and I couldn't obey.

I vividly remember one particular instance during the time I was having the affair. I was driving to pick up Jake and Bryn at school and quoting to myself the Scripture, *Walk in the Spirit, and you shall not fulfill the lust of the flesh* (Galatians 5:16). But just when I was gaining strength from that truth, a raspy, rushed voice told me, "Yeah, but you can't always walk in the Spirit . . . and when you aren't, I'm gonna get you."

And I did again what I didn't want to do.

Why couldn't I stop messing up? Jesus lived in me. He had come and died on the cross to permanently do away with sin. I cried. I repented. I felt guilty. I patched up the cracks in the armor and repolished it. And then I tried again with another "key" verse . . . the promises of which I again couldn't claim because of my disobedience.

But in all of this struggle, I had failed to trace the question one step farther back. I had not asked: What makes obedience possible? How was it that *as a man* Jesus chose perfect submission at all times? What was the foundation of Jesus' obedience?

Thanks to the continued trials that kept pushing me deeper into God for the purging of the lies, I now understand the answer to those questions.

Jesus remained in unbroken obedience because He knew the Father's perfect and complete love. Belief in God's love enabled Jesus to stay in constant relationship with His Father. Pure and simple, everything Jesus did was possible because deep in the core of His humanity, He knew that God loved Him. He trusted in that love so much that He humbled Himself in total obedience to it.

How did Jesus come to this place of rest—this position of complete trust in the total love of the Father?

He simply believed God's Word was unshakably true.

At the start of His earthly ministry, when Jesus was baptized in the river Jordan, the Father spoke from heaven directly to Him: *And suddenly a voice came from heaven, saying, "This is* ***My beloved Son,*** *in whom I am well pleased"* (Matthew 3:17).

On the Mount of Transfiguration, the Father addressed Him again: *This is **My beloved Son,** in whom I am well pleased* (Matthew 17:5). The Father called Jesus, "My beloved Son." The words are for Jesus and all the world to hear.

And Jesus received this powerful and perfect Word from His Father. He *knew* He was the "beloved Son." In the most profound sense, Jesus knew God's love in the core of His being. He believed it despite the fact that up until the time He was baptized and the words were first spoken to Him, Jesus had done nothing extraordinary to "deserve" that love.

Jesus came to John to be baptized when He was about 30 years of age. Prior to that, as far as we know from Scripture, Jesus had done no miracles, taught no lessons and preached no messages. He had no higher education and was not well-traveled, wealthy or powerful. Rather, He had learned the simple trade of His earthly father—carpentry.

In His youth, He had displeased His parents and stayed behind in Jerusalem talking to the scribes in the temple. Prior to that, as a young child His incarnation had caused His parents great distress; because of Him they had fled to Egypt. And preceding that, He had been born in an animal shed in Bethlehem to an unwed, teenaged mother.

Yet despite these earthly circumstances, Jesus knew the Father loved Him. Soon after His baptism, He said, *The Father loves the Son* (John 3:35). And this knowledge of His Father's love expressed itself out in His life. Jesus' belief in God's love formed the basis for all He was and did. Jesus received the Father's love into Himself and let it pour forth; His life was love personified.

Jesus put Himself totally in God's hands because He trusted God's love for Him—even to the last drop of His *psuche* life. Trust and obedience were responses to the love He knew. Jesus chose to stay in God's will, even though that meant death on the cross, because He trusted in the love of God.

My mind had failed to grasp it before, but as I now understand it, Jesus knew God's perfect love, and it was living in that love that led Him into willing obedience. He surrendered the "I will" of Himself—His autonomous soul—because He knew the Father's love. Jesus' obedience came from resting in the security of His Father's love.

If you knew that Someone everywhere-present, all-knowing and all-powerful loved you unconditionally, wouldn't you trust Him too? Wouldn't you want Him to guide you? God is omnipresent, omniscient, omnipotent *and* all-loving; that's an unbeatable recipe for trust.

Think about it. If you were a blind man attempting to climb a steep cliff, wouldn't you trust and follow the leading of a guide who you were confident really loved you?

A few years ago, Floyd, my almost-blind friend, climbed a shale cliff to reach the pinnacled top of a mountain in the Sierras. At the peak, Pastor Andy and tall, strong Carl guided his hands and feet to crevices in the rock face so he could pull himself up. Floyd trusted Andy and Carl that much because he knew they really loved him.

Love brings trust. Psalm 36:7 says, *How precious is Your lovingkindness, O God! Therefore the children of men put their trust under the shadow of Your wings.*

Trust comes naturally as we learn of God's love. An increasing understanding of God's love for us brings trust, surrender, obedience and humility . . . which brings us back again to increasing love. It is an endless cycle of growing in humility and love.

Jesus knew the fullness of the Father's endless love. Over and over again, He makes reference to it: *The Father loved Me* (John 15:9); *You have loved Me* (John 17:23); *You loved Me* (John 17:26).

And because Jesus trusted that love, He gave up everything of Himself and embraced all that the Father had to give—all His will, His ways, His power, His character, His very essence . . . Himself. Thus, everything of God came into Jesus. God's love came to earth in Jesus Christ.

And that love came *through* Jesus to us!

The entirety of the Scriptures just quoted above are as follows:

As the Father loved Me, I also have loved you (John 15:9).

I in them, and You in Me; that they may be made perfect in one, and that the world may know that You have sent Me, and ***have loved them as You have loved Me*** (John 17:23).

And I have declared to them Your name, and will declare it, ***that the love with which You loved Me may be in them,*** *and I in them* (John 17:26).

As the Son of Man, Jesus believed in the Father's lavish love . . . and passed that love on to us! Jesus' knowing the Father's love came first; His love for us followed from that. As the Son of Man, Jesus loved us with the Father's love.

Like Jesus, I too was meant to know the Father's love and pass it on to others. I too was created to be an unbroken watercourse of His light, life and love. We were made to be recipients and sharers of God's great love.

But we have to believe in the love. Unless we believe in it, it is as if it doesn't exist for us.

In order to love others, I had to believe how much God loved me.

Part Six

Soul Wars: Believing in God's Done Deal

Jesus accomplished everything—the complete restoration of our spirit, soul and body. But I had not realized the fullness of the New Covenant life He had modeled and made possible for us.

Indeed, some of the Bible's most powerful Scriptures about life and love were tainted by my unrenewed mind, colored by Satan's same old lies.

If I were going to love others like He first loved me, I had to cast off those lies and believe how much He actually, really did love me.

CHAPTER 19

Lies About Love

The bottom line is that our souls were created to know the love of God. When we know God's love, our broken hearts are healed, and we are set free to love others as He first loved us.

So, all I have to do is believe in God's infinite love for me. . . .

But that isn't as easy as it sounds.

Satan is "the father of lies." The feelings, thoughts and behaviors that we know aren't right in ourselves and the sins and weights we see in others are by-products of the lies he has flung like fiery darts at our minds. "The deceiver of the brethren" has broken our hearts, put us in prison and blinded us to the love of God.

Satan knows that our believing in God's love will be his demise, so he shoots lies about God's love into our minds. It's impossible for Satan to prevent God from loving us, so instead he tries to prevent us from believing that He does. If we don't believe in God's love, it's like it isn't there for us. We can live our lives oblivious to God's love even though it's all around us.

Of course, at some level, I understood that God loved me; the lie was subtle and deceptive. I could quote the Bible verses. I knew His love in my spirit; I was born again. And that night in church when God had poured His love down upon me from the center of the cross was unforgettable.

But somehow I didn't know God's love in my innermost mind—in the core of my being—way down in my soul. And because I didn't know it deep in my soul, I wasn't living it out. I wasn't accepting His will and way as my own so that His light, life and love bubbled up and out of me from within.

Deep inside of me the old song still played: *He's making a list. He's checking it twice. He's gonna find out if you're naughty or nice.* In the core of my being, I somehow believed the way of Santa Claus, the way of our parents and our parents' parents, to be the way of our heavenly Father.

Jesus came to break the Forbidden Tree mindset, but the seed of that wrong way of thinking has deep roots. I still had a long way to go to be free from the system in which the elevated soul, with its knowledge of good and evil, contaminated my thinking telling me that I needed to be good to earn God's love. The deception is hundreds of generations thick and must be peeled off layer by layer, clear back to Adam.

Each one of us deals with some derivative of the same basic lie that God doesn't love us. Although it may be so well hidden beneath the veneer of conscious thought that we can't admit it's there, that doesn't make its presence any less real. Regardless of gender, race, age or religious beliefs, the misconception has the same root: *God doesn't love me because . . .*

A few years ago at a church potluck, I was sitting at a table with David, the piano player and math teacher. He started talking about the basic lie he had believed. David is an only child whose parents were divorced when he was 5. From earliest memory, David had believed a lie similar to the one I had held. He thought if he didn't perform, he wouldn't be accepted and loved. But from there, his deception took a different twist. David felt he was inadequate to perform and consequently was unloved and deserving of death. Therefore, rather than constantly working to try to receive love as I had done, David was prone to depression, withdrawal and giving up.

In talking to Naomi, Pastor Andy's wife, I learned that the lie she had believed reflected the turmoil she experienced in early life. Her father was having an affair during the time of Naomi's conception and wanted his wife to abort baby Naomi. In her young life, uncaring stepfathers and quarreling older sisters further reinforced Naomi's feelings of being an unwanted burden. She felt confused, that she had nothing to offer, that she was worthless . . . and generally unlovable.

My friend Jill with the thick, dark hair held in her core a lie that wasn't exactly clear. Her older parents had been trying to have children for some time when Jill, her brother and her sister were conceived as triplets. Jill's sister died in the womb, and her parents worried excessively that the same thing would happen to the other babies. Jill grew up feeling that she might die and wanting to die to end the worry over dying. She believed something was the matter with her, that she couldn't be herself and that she should have done more to help her sister. Behind this flood of emotions and wrong thinking lurked the underlying lie that if God really loved her, none of this would have happened.

Christopher, who helped me greatly in writing and editing this book, had yet a different derivation of the lie. Christopher comes from a strong Christian family. To him it seemed that his parents loved him—that is, he felt they loved what they knew of him. But deep down, Christopher thought that if they really knew who he was and saw the evil hidden within, they wouldn't love him. He believed anybody who really knew his flaws, like God did, couldn't possibly love him.

God knows all about these lies and the associated hurts, negative thoughts and wrong behaviors they generate. He came to take them away so that we could live in freedom—open and honest, totally known and loved by our awesome God.

But Satan will try to block us from that love in any way he can . . . even by causing us to wrongly interpret Scripture.

Some of the most potent deceptions that fed the basic lie I believed had to do with New Covenant Scriptures that I interpreted with an Old Covenant mentality. They related to Tree of Life promises that I misunderstood because of a Forbidden Tree mindset. Repeatedly, the New Testament speaks of a relationship between love and keeping His commandments. But because of the foundational lie I had believed—that God would love me if I were good, but if I behaved badly, He wouldn't—I'd completely misinterpreted that connection.

Until recently I couldn't even explain my wrong thinking. The lie was garbled so I did not know exactly what I thought. It was like billowing smoke obscured the deception so I was unable to see it clearly. But now that ugly lie is exposed.

Let me explain. In my distorted understanding, my obedience was a prerequisite for God's love.

In John 14, Jesus tells us:

If you ***love*** *Me, you will* ***keep My commandments.***

He who has ***My commandments and keeps*** *them is the one who* ***loves*** *Me; and he who* ***loves*** *Me will be* ***loved*** *by My Father.*

If anyone ***loves*** *Me, he will* ***keep My word;*** *and My Father will* ***love*** *him* (John 14:15, 21, 23, NASB).

In the New International Version (the one I had stored in my deep mind), the word **"keep"** is translated **obey.** *If you **love** Me, you will **obey** . . .*

From earliest memory, I had interpreted these Scriptures as saying, "Mary, if you really love me, you will be good. You will prove your love for me by being obedient. Just obey the Ten Commandments. Then I'll know you love me."

"And if I know you love me," the false interpretation continued, "then I will love you too and so will my father. Come on. You can do it. I'm rooting for you. I want to love you. Just obey my commands and be good so that I can."

I am not capitalizing "me," "my" or "father" in the above interpretation because this was obviously not Holy Spirit truth.

Under the deception, love was something I had to work for by being obedient. It started with me—with my good behavior. If I kept His commandments, that would prove that I loved God. And if I loved God, then He would love me in return. Thus, under the lie, I believed I could earn His love by proving, through my good deeds, that I loved Him.

But there was a major problem. I could never be obedient enough to make the lie-based system work. Sometimes I did things I knew were wrong, but when I was very good, pride welled up in me, and that definitely wasn't good. Thus, I felt I could never attain God's love because no matter how hard I tried, I couldn't obey His commandments. The proper behaviors weren't in me.

As part of this lie, I viewed obedience as something a harsh master might demand of a cowering servant. It came with a you-must-do-it feeling. Inherent in the obedience was a just-do-it-on-the-surface pressure to perform. The picture I had stored in my head was one of a prison guard, muscled and mean, imposing conformity to the laws of the prison upon a jailed inmate. It was a forced type of obedience based on fear.

But my understanding was so, so distorted.

When Jesus said, *If you* ***love*** *Me, you will* ***keep My commandments.*** *. . . He who has* ***My commandments and keeps*** *them is the one who* ***loves*** *Me; and he who* ***loves*** *Me will be* ***loved*** *by My Father. . . . If anyone loves Me, he will* ***keep My word;*** *and My Father will* ***love*** *him* (John 14:15, 21, 23, NASB), He is describing a completely different system from the one I had wrongly assumed.

First, the meaning of the word "commandments" is not the one I had believed it to be. When I saw the words "My commandments," I automatically thought of the Ten Commandments. But that is not what Jesus is referring to. As Gaylord aptly points out in his book, *Love Revolution,* "commandment<u>s</u>" or "command<u>s</u>" refers to those radiating out of the one "new commandment": *A* ***new commandment*** *I give to you, that you love one another; as I have loved you, that you also love one another* (John 13:34). The "new commandment" (singular) is the command from which all others (plural) spring.

Later, Jesus repeats it for clarity. *If you keep My* ***commandment<u>s</u>,*** *you will abide in My love. . . . This is my* ***commandment,*** *that you love one another as I have loved you* (John 15:10, 12).

Second, neither is His definition of the word "keep" or "obey" like the one I had held. The Greek word for "keep" or "obey" is *tereo.* As Gaylord also makes clear, *tereo* actually means to guard from loss by keeping the eye upon.

Tereo has none of the connotation of a harsh prison guard imposing rules on an inmate. Rather, the image this word conjures up in my mind is one of a gentle, wise grandpa speaking to a child on his lap. "Please," he says, "stay in my love. Value my love so much that you never let it out of your sight. Treasure and guard it in your heart. It is the best for you."

And in my image the little girl looks up into her grandpa's loving eyes and nods her head in agreement. She trusts her adoring grandpa's words. It is an obedience that arises naturally from the child's knowing that her grandpa loves her.

Obedience comes as a spirit-natural consequence of knowing we are loved. Obedience flows from God's love in us. In this sense, "If you love Me, you will obey . . ." is parallel to saying, "If you run a marathon, you will be tired." Just like fatigue comes as a natural consequence of running, obedience comes as a natural consequence of knowing we are loved.

God's love for us doesn't start with our obedience; our obedience starts with knowing God's love. If we don't know He loves us despite our sin, we will hide like Adam and Eve did and be afraid to come to Him. But love opens the door for us to bring Him our true selves . . . so He can deliver a real cure. *God's kindness is intended to lead you to repent [to change your mind and inner man to accept God's will]* (Romans 2:4, Amplified).

From back in high school, I remember a quote Mama had handwritten and pasted onto the refrigerator: *God doesn't love us because we are good; He makes us good because He loves us.*

Back then, 30-plus years ago, I wasn't sure if the statement were correct or not, but I desperately wanted it to be true.

Now I know it's a fact.

We will be like Him when we see Him as He really is (full of love for us), not when we try to make ourselves into loving creatures by doing commendable deeds. God doesn't want me fooling around and trying to deal with my disobedience my way by hiding and suppressing it behind a shiny-armor façade. He wants me to trust Him so He can dig out the lies—the root cause of the bad fruit—and replace them with the pure truth of His love for me.

We love, because He first loved us (1 John 4:19, NASB). Receiving precedes giving. The Father's love pours into us as we believe in it. And as we accept God's love, we have love to give away. We can't give what we don't have. We can only love one another as He first loved us. And when we do that, we are obeying His one command. It's so simple, so pure, so freeing.

When we love others, we demonstrate in real life—we make visible to the world—our love for God. Scripture tells us, *He who does not love his brother whom he has seen, how can he love God whom he has not seen?* (1 John 4:20). We love Him by loving one another. Jesus said, *Inasmuch as you did it to one of the least of these My brethren, you did it to Me* (Matthew 25:40).

And so in the way God designed it, love just keeps growing on itself. In God's love system, we never come to the end of ever-increasing love. The Father's love for the Son and the world, the Son's love for the Father and us, the Holy Spirit's love for me and others, my love for others and Jesus—all these are the same love and all keep expanding as we give and receive in relationship.

Now I see that the John 14 Scriptures are simply a description of how God designed things to be under the New Covenant. These Scriptures are not telling me what I must *do* to earn love. Rather, they are a beautiful description of how God designed things to *be* in relationship.

In God's system, love isn't *attained* by doing; it is *shared* in relationship.

When abiding in love, we become loving creatures. Under the New Covenant, God supplies the love that makes us able to love others. The New Covenant provides for us to live in the love-rest of God—where the command to love fulfills itself as part of His promise to us who believe in His love. In that love-rest, *doing* flows from *being* as naturally as water flows from a spring. Good deeds come forth from God's love in our souls as naturally as good fruit grows on a good tree.

In John 15, Jesus gives an explanation of the fruit-bearing, life-giving love relationship He intends for us:

> *I am the vine, you are the branches. He who abides in Me, and I in him, bears much fruit; for without Me you can do nothing. . . . By this My Father is glorified, that you bear much fruit; so you will be My disciples. As the Father loved Me, I also have loved you; abide in My love. If you keep My commandments, you will abide in My love, just as I have kept My Father's commandments and abide in His love* (John 15:5, 8-10).

In these words, I hear Jesus pleading: "Please. Come and abide in Me. Come and live in My love just like I lived in My Father's love. Believe in My love for you like I believed in the Father's love for Me. You can't do it alone. We designed you for love relationship with Us. Please. Just embrace My love for you . . . then you can love others . . . and we can share love together."

In Ephesians 3:14, 17-19, Paul prays that we might know the love of Christ:

> *For this reason I bow my knees to the Father . . . that you, being rooted and grounded in love, may be able to comprehend with all the saints what is the width and length and depth and height—to know the love of Christ which passes knowledge; that you may be filled with all the fullness of God.*

We are "rooted and grounded in love" . . . so that we can grasp its extent . . . so that we can know even more of Christ's love. The challenge before us is to "comprehend" the love of Christ. "All the fullness of God" comes from knowing the boundless expanse of His love.

In the Amplified Bible, the last part of Ephesians 3:19 reads, . . . *that you may be filled [through all your being] unto all the fullness of God [may have the richest measure of the divine Presence, and become a body wholly filled and flooded with God Himself]!* Deep in the core of our inner man—in our personality, our soul—we were meant to be "filled and flooded" with the love of God.

God's desire is that we be filled in spirit, soul and body with His love and thereby come to our completion as human beings.

However, for most of my adulthood, I had been struggling to live a "good Christian" life of a completely different nature. I thought God's purpose and will for me involved something else entirely.

CHAPTER 20

STRIVINGS OF THE SOUL

Because of the foundational lie I had held—that God would love me if I were good, but if I behaved badly He wouldn't—I had not seen life for what it really was. I'd thought our purpose in life was to do good deeds (as I defined them) and avoid evil and that Jesus had come to help us do that. I believed that God wanted me to live a sinless, holy life as defined essentially by the Old Covenant, with Jesus added into the mix to make that possible. I somehow assumed that with Christ in me, I would be strengthened to consistently choose good, thereby fulfilling the Old Covenant requirements.

I used to believe I as a Christian was called to fight the battle diagrammed in Figure 20-A. In that battle, "I" was in the middle being pulled in a vicious tug-of-war between good and evil.

It seemed this model of "Christian life" had been taught to me in Sunday school and preached to me in sermons year after year. Time and time again, I was admonished to press on in choosing good over evil. Under this distortion, I defined "the victorious Christian life" as one in which good was continually chosen while evil was continually shunned.

The personal struggle Paul describes at the end of Romans chapter 7 portrays the battle I believed was mine to fight as a "good Christian." For most of my life I have felt the weight of Paul's words: *For the good that **I will** to do, I do not do; but the evil **I will** not to do, that I practice* (Romans 7:19). Paul wants to do good, but evil pulls him off course, and he ends up doing that instead.

In agonizing detail, Paul paints a picture of the tumultuous battle of the "I" of himself—his soul—to do good and avoid evil. In verses 15 to 24, Paul uses the word "I" 23 times. His focus is on the good the "I" must do and the evil the "I" must avoid. Paul is stuck on thinking about himself . . . despite the fact that "I will" is completely unable to muster the desired good. The autonomous soul is incapable of good; good does not exist apart from God.

Paul is in a bad way and he knows it. At the end of the chapter, he cries out, *O **wretched** man that I am! Who will deliver me from this body of death?* (Romans 7:24).

The word "wretched" used here does not refer to a cruel or worthless person. It is not a term that would be used to define the character of a drunk lying in the gutter. Paul is not struggling against evil in that sense. Rather, the word "wretched" comes from the Greek word *talaiporos,* which means miserably weighted down from work. Trying to do commendable deeds has exhausted Paul. He is heavy-laden with overwork.

Until recently, that was my wretched state as well.

For years and years as a Christian, before getting MS, I worked hard to do what I felt was good. In my mind, I was a good mother to Jake, Bryn, Anne and Mark. We went to church and Bible studies. Through research I was helping out malnourished children in Kenya. I was emotionally and financially supporting Dennis through the grueling years of residency.

I was master of my own ship. I did what I wanted to do. But because the things I chose were highly commendable, I, and most everyone around me it seemed, assumed they were what God was after. Like a modern-day Pharisee, I did the good my soul, working under its own authority and *psuche* strength, chose to do. And so I lived my Christian life oblivious to the truth and without real peace and freedom.

The form and structure of the Christian teaching I had grown up with had imposed themselves upon my soul. As a consequence, without my realizing it, my soul had come to define "good" and "evil" based upon church standards and then tried to do that good in its own strength. And when my "good Christian" soul didn't conform and something I knew was evil sprang forth, I tried desperately to hide it behind more good.

I did not know then that sin in God's definition is running your own ship—with the autonomous soul leading the way. It is doing things (regardless of how commendable those things appear) apart from life-giving relationship with God.

When I got MS, however, I couldn't do the good anymore. My flesh didn't have the strength. I couldn't even care for my own children. And just when I was adjusting to life with my doing of commendable deeds pruned back to a level manageable with the MS, I did the consummate evil in my rule book and had an affair. For that I condemned myself, put on more rules and then, gathering strength, pushed back to the good side of the Forbidden Tree once again. Of course, I was doing all this as a born-again believer. Because I was saved, I just assumed I was doing it right. . . .

Until God halted me through Edna's words, "Mary, you don't love."

Now I know that we were not created to live life fighting Paul's battle. Paul describes the battle in order to show us the wretched state we are *not* to live in. The battle that consumes Paul at the end of Romans chapter 7 describes the struggle of the believer, fighting with all the strength the autonomous soul can muster, to fulfill the requirements of the Old Covenant. Paul is saved in his spirit (see Romans 7:22), but his mind is stuck in the bondage of Old Covenant thought.

Jesus did not come to help us win that battle. He came to set us free by lifting us out of it. He elevates us out of the Old Covenant way of knowing what is good and evil and trying to do that good in our own strength. His desire is to lift us into New Covenant life in the love-rest of God. In that love-rest, we function not as beings governed by our independent souls, but as people governed by the Holy Spirit through our spirit. We rest in the fullness of God.

For Paul and for us New Covenant believers, the battle between good and evil is only a sham fight. Like a carefully scripted professional wrestling match, it looks convincing on the surface, but it is not the life we are called to live. Everything under the Forbidden Tree spells death. The good is just as wrong as the evil, only more deceptive.

Satan will do anything to keep us from entering the love-rest of God. One of his favorite tactics is to cause us Christians to focus our attention on good versus evil, thus blinding us to God's way altogether. Satan would have us spend our time and energies engaged in a battle in which, regardless of the good or evil outcome, we are separated from God and His love.

God did not design the soul to rally itself and muster up commendable deeds. Love isn't something produced like a commendable deed by the autonomous soul. God designed the soul to surrender its will and live by way of the Spirit—by way of *zoe* life. Love is meant to flow from God's love in us, translated through our souls, to the world.

God desires that we step out from the bondage of the Old Covenant way and live in the freedom and rest of the New. We do that with a born-again spirit *and* with a renewed mind—a purified soul. God wants us to stop thinking with an Old Covenant/Tree of Knowledge mindset and enter fully into the life-giving love relationship that Jesus offers as the Tree of Life.

As I now understand it, the true picture of the choice before us is shown in Figure 20-B. In this diagram, there are two separate systems—the way of the Tree of Life and the way of the Tree of the Knowledge of Good and Evil. God's desire is that we step out from fighting the in-the-flesh battle under the Old Covenant and embrace the in-the-Spirit life of the New.

The Spirit and the flesh are at war. "In the Spirit" is about being in relationship with God. "In the Spirit" is letting the Holy Spirit in our spirit have His will in the "I" of us—in our soul. "In the Spirit" we don't have to worry about *doing* at all. "In the Spirit" is about *being* in relationship with God.

"In the flesh," on the other hand, is about operating from a source outside of relationship with God. Anything powered and directed by the autonomous soul with its knowledge of good and evil is done "in the flesh." The term refers to the nature of man being guided by himself without the Holy Spirit. Romans 8:3 in the Amplified Bible makes this clear: *For God has done what the Law could not do, [its power] being weakened by* ***the flesh [the entire nature of man without the Holy Spirit].*** Anything done "in the flesh" is carried out in the strength of *psuche* life alone.

The Spirit and the flesh are engaged in a monumental tug-of-war for the soul of the believer. The Spirit calls the mind, will and emotions of the soul to line up with God. By this, we become truly good. But the flesh—the soul and body of us apart from the Holy Spirit—urges us to act autonomously and do good (or evil) apart from God.

The decision for the soul is between living a life in God that is truly good or living a life striving to be like God by doing good deeds and avoiding evil ones. The defining question is: Will the "I" humble itself, give up its authority and trust in the love of God to bring forth what is truly good? The battle isn't to do good deeds; it is to become good by entering the love-rest of God.

In Romans chapter 8, Paul chooses the way of the Spirit. His "I" battle of Romans 7 ceases, and he rests in God. Victorious, he breaks into freedom proclaiming, *I thank God—through Jesus Christ our Lord! . . . There is therefore now no condemnation to those who are in Christ Jesus. For the law of the Spirit of life in Christ Jesus has made me free from the law of sin and death* (Romans 7:25-8:2).

Paul has chosen the way of the Tree of Life. He has surrendered the autonomy of his soul, turned from its constant struggle to do good deeds and embraced the fullness of the life God provides us as Spirit-ruled beings.

I used to read these passages and look for Paul's transformation toward becoming a "sinless and holy" man as I defined those terms—by living a life doing only good deeds. But Scripture does not show us this type of transformation. Paul does not say, "Praise God, now I am continually choosing to do good things." Paul is not even thinking about "good" and "evil" as defined by the Old Covenant Law and how he may or may not measure up.

Rather, Scripture shows us a change in Paul's mindset. He no longer thinks about himself, the good he must do and the evil he must shun. Now his gaze is upon Christ. Paul is truly becoming a righteous man—not by focusing on himself and his behaviors but by looking to God. *I thank God—through Jesus Christ our Lord!* Paul joyfully proclaims.

Just as with Paul, that change in focus will move us as believers into the fullness of the life God designed for us. Through us, with our minds set on Christ, all creation will be set free into the *zoe* life of God (see Romans 8:19, 21).

I'm only now beginning to comprehend. . . .

For so long I'd boxed Jesus up and stuck Him into my structure—into my way of thinking and being formed by the beliefs I'd held since babyhood growing up with Mama and Daddy in our all-American, Christian home. I'd asked Him, begged Him, pleaded with Him to help me choose to do good deeds (all the while refusing the love that would make me truly good, because I didn't think I deserved it.).

But Jesus hadn't come to help me run my life that way. He had come to transform my mind and purify my soul so that the framework of my being could embrace the fullness of God and His love for me.

Since that day at Edna's, I've learned slowly, through the trials coupled with the ongoing counseling, a more excellent way. God just wants me to jump with both feet into His love.

Our only striving is to cease struggling to live life the Old Covenant way. Scripture tells us, *For he who has once entered [God's] rest also has ceased from [the weariness and pain] of human labors. . . . Let us therefore be zealous and exert ourselves and strive diligently to enter that rest* (Hebrews 4:10-11, Amplified).We rest in His finished work and believe that He loves us extravagantly. We humble ourselves to His way and let His love pour through us to accomplish His purpose.

Romans chapter 8 ends with a promise: *Neither death nor life, nor angels nor principalities nor powers, nor things present nor things to come, nor height nor depth, nor any other created thing, shall be able to separate us from the love of God which is in Christ Jesus our Lord* (Romans 8:38-39).

Nothing can separate us from His love. We get to dwell in it, rest in it and live out the transforming power of it to others.

Wow! What joy! What freedom!

All I have to do is believe and enter into the love-rest of God.

But that's difficult. It's hard to stop thinking in the mindset of the lies.

And because God knew it wouldn't be easy, He gave us warnings and stories about just that topic . . . peppered in love.

FIGURE 20

STRIVINGS OF THE SOUL

A. PAUL'S ROMANS 7 BATTLE: DOING GOOD

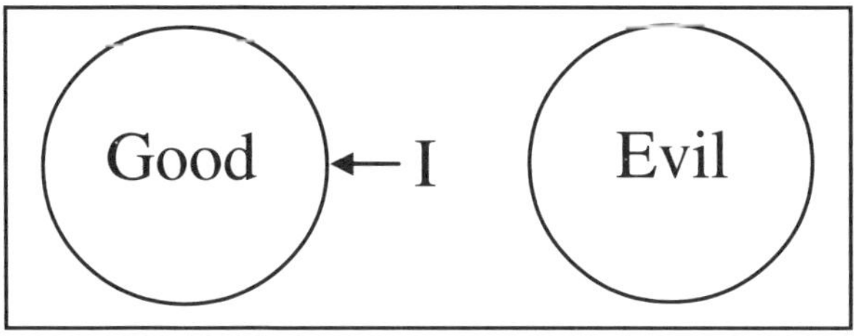

B. PAUL'S ROMANS 8 VICTORY: LIVING IN THE LOVE OF GOD

Tree of Life

Tree of Knowledge of Good and Evil

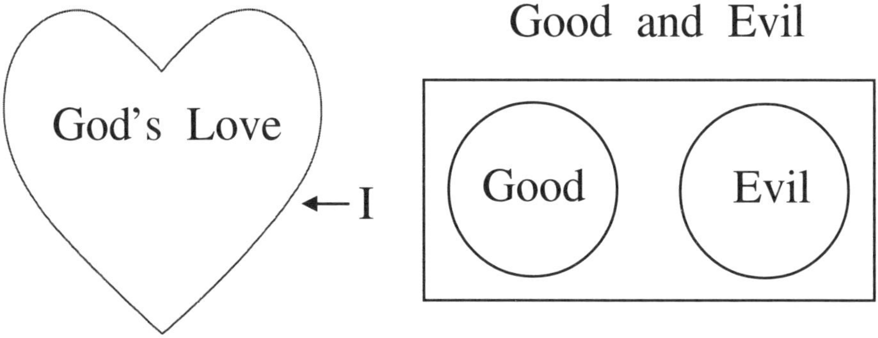

"In the Spirit"

"In the flesh"

CHAPTER 21

Prodigals and Older Brothers

Over and over again, the writers of the New Testament warn of falling back into the Old Covenant way and doing things outside of relationship with God. They repeatedly alert us to the dangers of living life doing "good" as defined by the Forbidden Tree.

Second Timothy 3:5 speaks of *having a form of godliness but denying its power.* The form is there; things look commendable on the surface. But the substance—the power in Christ—is lacking.

Paul admonishes the early Christians: *O foolish Galatians! Who has bewitched you that you should not obey the truth?. . . Are you so foolish? Having begun in the Spirit, are you now being made perfect by the flesh?* (Galatians 3:1, 3). The Galatians, too, were being tempted to fall back on commendable deeds and do things the Old Covenant way.

But of all the passages contrasting the Old Covenant system with the New, the story of the prodigal son and the older brother is my favorite. In this story, both the sons are operating in the mentality of the Old Covenant, but the father is firmly functioning in the schema of the New.

The sons are caught up in thinking about their own personal good and evil behaviors and the perceived consequences of those actions. They are focused on the rewards/punishments and love/withholding of love they think they deserve based on their behaviors. Both sons have a "doing" mentality; they see acceptance, blessings and love as rewards to be achieved or withheld based on what they have done.

The prodigal son knows he has done wrong. Based on this, he considers himself undeserving of blessing and love. He comes back to his father and says, *I have sinned against heaven and in your sight, and am no longer worthy to be called your son* (Luke 15:21). He does not think himself deserving of his father's love because he has sinned. Forbidden Tree thinking causes him to wrongly believe his deeds define his worth. Under the Old Covenant Law, he would be cursed, so he condemns himself and assumes that his father does too.

On the other hand, the older brother judges himself to have done good things. Based on this, he considers himself worthy of blessing and love. But he doesn't feel he has been adequately rewarded with these—at least in comparison to his undeserving brother. He tells his father, *Lo, these many years I have been serving you; I never transgressed your commandment at any time; and yet you never gave me a young goat, that I might make merry with my friends* (Luke 15:29).

A Forbidden Tree mentality causes the older brother to assume that his good behaviors have qualified him to receive his father's blessings. It upsets him that his wayward brother is enjoying what he does not feel is deserved. Under the Old Covenant system, it is he, the older, hardworking son, who should have earned blessings.

Both sons have got life wrong. Their thinking is based on a Tree of Knowledge of Good and Evil mentality. And they assume the way they think of themselves is the way their father thinks of them.

In actuality, however, the father judges neither of his children on the basis of their behavior. He is operating with a Tree of Life mentality and simply wants to have a loving relationship with both.

The father welcomes the prodigal home with open arms. He sees him coming and runs to embrace and kiss him. He dresses him up and throws a celebration for him. He is filled with joy because his son—his son who was "dead" and "lost"—has come home to live with him.

With equal ardor, the father also loves the older son. He assures him that whatever he has belongs to him. He invites the hardworking son into the party too, so that he can be close to him as well. He assures him, *Son, you are always with me, and all that I have is yours* (Luke 15:31).

How the sons view themselves—working or wandering, worthy or worthless—is irrelevant. Both sons are on equal footing with the father. All he wants is a loving relationship with each. Blessings and inheritance are meant for both sons regardless of past behaviors.

The issue of monumental import has nothing to do with past behaviors. It has everything to do with present choice. Will the wandering son choose to accept the love the father is offering? Will the working son choose to accept it? Will the sons choose to be in relationship with their father?

The dynamic in the story is provided not by how much love the father is able to give, but by how much love each son is willing to receive. How much of the father's love can each of the sons believe belongs to them?

How much of the Father's love can I believe belongs to me? How much of the Father's love can you believe belongs to you?

The dynamic in my life is provided by how much I believe in the Father's love for me—by how much love I am able to receive.

One of the quotes I have copied into the front of my Bible says, *The greatest of saints is simply the greatest of receivers.*

Yes! Belief in God's love—and the rich inheritance He gives us because of His love—is the key to receiving it. And once we receive that love and inheritance, we can extend it to others.

But I hadn't really accepted God's love for me. Rather, I had been thinking like a jumbled combination of the two sons. When I knew I'd done wrong, I was like the prodigal, returning to the Father in amazement that He would take me back and want a relationship with me. But when I was hardworking and did commendable things, I believed myself to be, in some way, deserving of a piece of the Father's love.

Before the affair, I'd been like the hardworking older son. I had done things I considered good and worthy of love. And I'd assumed He loved me because of that. Pride told me I was deserving.

But what I was receiving as the older brother wasn't really the Father's love at all. Rather, it was my own ill-conceived notion of God's acceptance. I obviously hadn't known much of His love, or I would never have had the affair in an attempt to fill that love void in the first place.

After the affair I'd been, for a while, like the prodigal son. I couldn't believe God could love a sinner like me. I didn't like myself and therefore I believed, in some distorted way, that God didn't like me either. Thus, I was condemned by my own twisted mindset.

But I pushed back again to the good side of the Forbidden Tree and continued on.

Living life flip-flopping back and forth between good and evil was very stressful. When I behaved badly, condemnation came like engulfing black night. But when I did commendable deeds, pride welled up like swirling white smoke.

And no matter how hard I tried, I never could do the good anyway. Regardless of how many hours I prayed and read my Bible, no matter how devoted a mother I was or how many hours I worked for the wonderful causes of helping starving children in Kenya or spreading the Gospel in India . . . I couldn't do enough. My strength wasn't sufficient.

I couldn't love like the Old Covenant Law told me I should. It was impossible to love God with all that was in me and have any left over for my neighbor. And loving my neighbor like I loved myself didn't work because I didn't love myself. How could I love myself when I wasn't sure God loved me (because I couldn't do the things I felt were required to deserve that love)?

And so I flip-flopped back and forth, blind to the fact that life as I knew it was fundamentally different from the one God had designed me to enjoy. Somehow I held on to the false hope that one day I would find a way to become good enough to reach God's love and all His promises.

But that day at Edna's, I knew I had gotten the whole thing wrong. I was failing miserably at the most important thing—loving. My good behaviors were never going to get me there. They weren't designed to.

Looking back on it now, I had been living the Christian life with one foot in the Old Covenant and one foot in the New. My spirit was saved, but the eternal life of God hadn't flooded my soul. My spirit was clearly functioning in the New; the Holy Spirit lived in me. But my mind was still thinking with the mentality of the Old.

I hadn't stepped into the finished work of Christ for the renewing of my mind. My thinking about God and myself wasn't in line with God's Word. I hadn't believed fully in God's love for me.

Jesus' disciples came to Him asking, *What shall we do, that we may work the works of God?* (John 6:28). And Jesus responded, *This is the work of God, that you* ***believe*** *in Him whom He sent* (John 6:29).

That is all He wants us to do—believe.

The other day in church, we sang the song *Only Believe*. David thumped out the melody on the piano, adding all sorts of frills as he went along. Carl tilted his head back, raised his left hand and sang to heaven. Naomi went with the flow and added extra "only believes" when David's improvising of the song called for it.

Only believe.
Only believe.
All things are possible.
Only believe.

Indeed, all of our becoming who God created us to be is wrapped up in our believing in Him and in His love. Belief connects us to the reality of who He is.

Faith believes the love behind all God's dealings with us. It is the key to bringing God's promises to life. *Faith is the substance of things hoped for . . .* (Hebrews 11:1). *And this is the victory that has overcome the world—our faith* (1 John 5:4). When we believe in His great love for us, all His promises to us come alive.

As I read Scripture, the deep truth of His love for me sinks in: *Because of His great love with which He loved us, even when we were dead in trespasses, [He] made us alive together with Christ . . . and raised us up together, and made us sit together in the heavenly places in Christ Jesus* (Ephesians 2:4-6). Because of His love, we are seated with Christ in heavenly places!

First John 4:16-17 says, *We have come to know and have* ***believed the love*** *which God has for us. God is love, and the one who abides in love abides in God, and God abides in him. By this,* ***love is perfected with us,*** *so that we may have confidence in the day of judgment;* ***because as He is, so also are we in this world*** (NASB).

I asked Jill one time what she thought those verses meant. She looked right at me and said, "Mary, they mean exactly what they say."

Wow! When we believe in God's awesome love for us—when "love is perfected with us"—we will be like Jesus in this world!

I want to believe in all of God's love for me. I will never come to the end of knowing His infinite love, but the wonderful thing is, I get to keep living in more and more of it every day.

We all do. We were created to be part of His glorious cure!

Part Seven

Living the Solution

We as humans are meant to live as participants in the great solution. Simply and purely, God intends for His love to completely fill and enliven our spirits, souls and bodies and pour out through us to heal a hurting world.

I'm stepping into the truth of that. My soul embraces the joy and freedom of living in the love-rest He has prepared for us.

CHAPTER 22

Bride Without Blemish

A few months ago, some of us from church went to hear a well-known Christian man who was speaking in the Sacramento area. The entire evening from start to finish was filled with God's presence. Extra folding chairs couldn't accommodate the crowd. People spilled out into the aisles and stood along the walls of the large auditorium. Worship was inspiring and the message delivered by this author and anointed man of God was full of truth.

At the end of the meeting, a group of young people were introduced. These men and women stood in the front and called out diseases or injuries people in the audience had that they believed God wanted to heal. "Numbness in the left shoulder." "Swelling and pain in both knees." "Deafness in the right ear."

As each condition was named, the individual or individuals suffering from that affliction raised his or her hand so that those around them could pray. God was moving powerfully. I left the service feeling blessed. God is awesome!

On the way home in the car that night with Pastor Andy, Naomi and Floyd, we began thinking. Many diseases had been specified for healing, but all had been diseases of the body—aches, pains and disabilities of the outer person. We could not recall anyone mentioning an affliction of the inner person.

No one, for example, had called out, "Freedom to forgive for one who was sexually assaulted." "Healing for a heart broken through the death of a child." "Wiping away the lie that God doesn't love you because your parents got a divorce."

No one had mentioned diseases of the soul.

But Jesus wants to heal our entire being—spirit, soul and body. He is coming back for a bride without spot, wrinkle or blemish, inside and out. He came to fully sanctify us, awaken us to His love and give us the full inheritance He intended us to have from the beginning.

Since the dark ages, the Church has been gradually recovering this truth. In the 1500s came a wave of grace for understanding what had been all but forgotten by the Church. God used Martin Luther as the point man for restoring to the Body of Christ the truth about believing in Jesus for eternal salvation.

The pious monk had been struggling for years with feelings of deep spiritual despair. Despite long hours in prayer, pilgrimage, frequent confessions and fasts, he had no assurance of salvation. Rather, increasing awareness of his own sinfulness plagued him.

Against this backdrop of hopelessness, Luther came to see the truth that salvation cannot be attained by works but is a free gift to be received by faith. As the story has been told, the German monk was climbing the monastery stairs on his knees trying, trying, trying to earn salvation through good works and proper penitence, when the words of Scripture came clearly to him, "The just shall live by faith."

Much of the Church now believes the truth that God, in His love, gives us salvation as a free gift. Thus, *zoe* life in the spirit is available. This treasure-truth of salvation has been unburied, and because of that, we in this generation can grasp it if we so choose. Today we know to believe for being born again. And when we believe, it happens; we *are* born again.

The truth that Christ's death paid the price for healing of the body began to trickle into Church thinking around the 1800s. Because of the work of many, including Kathryn Kuhlman, the woman I had so admired as a child, miraculous healing of the body is common today, especially in developing countries. In our present generation, the Church is increasingly embracing the truth that healing of the body is part of the finished work of Christ. We are coming to believe that God, in His love, gives us healing as a free gift. And as we believe that truth, it is becoming reality.

There remains, however, one last frontier—the soul. God wants to renew our mind, will and emotions. He lavishes the unconditional love that will mend our broken hearts and set us free to be the people He created us to be. Just as with eternal life and healing for the body, all we need do is believe in His love-provided cure.

Jesus said, *The Son of Man has come to seek and to **save** that which was lost* (Luke 19:10). That word "save" is from the Greek word *sozo. Sozo* refers to *all* the blessings bestowed by God on humanity. Jesus came to save every part of our being—spirit, soul and body. He enlivens the spirit by connecting Himself to us. He purifies the soul by filling it with His love truth, and He clothes the body in glory as it lives out that truth in the world. His salvation is full and complete, so that we can be fully and completely human.

"Salvation," the way we have come to use that term today, wonderful as it is, is just the beginning of the life God has planned for us. *Zoe* life is meant to sanctify us completely. Salvation is not just for the spirit part of us. We are meant to live in the love of God and become clean and spotless through and through. God intends that His love not only *dwells in us,* but also *flows up and out of us.*

This will happen as we believe. But before we can believe, we must know the truth of what to believe in. Hosea 4:6 says, *My people are destroyed for lack of knowledge.*

Until we grasp the truth of God's love for us and let that healing understanding permeate our souls, we will continue to make messes of our lives and of the world over which we were designed to rule and reign. I know because I personally was one of those mess-makers. Indeed, the history of the Church since the days of biblical times has been strewn with the mistakes people have made because of unhealed issues in the soul.

Men and women greatly used of God have been simultaneously used by the enemy to bring shame upon the Church. They have done this not because they weren't saved in their spirits, nor because of malicious intent. Rather, they fell into sins for the same reasons I had fallen and my life was a mess—-because we were unaware of God's provision for healing our souls. Thus, lies and hurts hidden deep inside festered to the surface and came out in horrible ways.

Martin Luther, for example, believed hateful ideas about the Jewish people. The last sermon he delivered three days before his death in 1546 was devoted to the need to cleanse German territory of Jews. And tragically, this thinking did not end with him. Four hundred years later, the Nazis used Luther's teachings as part of their justification for exterminating six million Jews.

Kathryn Kuhlman also suffered from unhealed issues in her soul. Hidden beneath flowing dresses and powerful healings was a struggling woman. Ms. Kuhlman knew this and asked that after her death, the behind-the-scenes account of her life be told. In a book titled *Daughter of Destiny: Kathryn Kuhlman . . . Her Story,* she bares her soul to us.

During the years as a prominent healing evangelist, Kuhlman lied repeatedly to the press about her divorce, her age and other aspects of her private life. She ran her ministry in a detached manner, dissociated and largely unknown even by her closest staff. Intense feelings of angst about letting God down plagued her.

Please hear my heart. I am not hanging out Kathryn Kuhlman's dirty laundry to degrade her. Ms. Kuhlman was connected with God in her spirit like few others in history, but she knew something wasn't right within. So rather than preserve a façade, she asked that the true story of her life be brought to light in the hope it would help others. In that, she left us a precious gift.

Please understand—Luther and Kuhlman were mighty warriors in their time. But their souls were contaminated with lies that tainted their life's work. In the core of their humanity, they somehow didn't know God's love.

I have heard it said that every revival in history came to an end because something of "man" got in. Theological divisions, sexual sins, big egos . . . whatever the cause, revival came to an end because something of "man"—something in the soul—shut it down. Souls not fulfilled in the love of God feel the need to seek satisfaction elsewhere or deaden the pain of unmet desire in hurtful ways.

Because of this, the pattern of the Church has been to have revival, conduct worship services and live out our Christian lives with as little of the "man" part of us as possible. We ask God for His external anointing so that

He might bypass us altogether. We are connected to God in our spirits, but we live out our lives in the world largely apart from that life-giving connection.

I know. I can relate. I functioned that way myself because I was unaware that God had created me to live differently.

Ms. Kuhlman did this too. Before her services she pleaded with God for His external anointing and wouldn't begin the healing part of the service until she knew He was present in that way. In a sense, it was as if Ms. Kuhlman believed God needed to work around her sinful self if He were going to accomplish His will. And God, by His grace, leaped over her clogged soul; powerful preaching and miraculous healings flowed from His external anointing.

In Old Testament times, before God came to live within, this bypassing of our humanity was necessary. But in this generation, we are not meant to operate like that. God intends that we function with the external anointing *and* with the internal bubbling up from within. He doesn't want to have to bypass us to bless others.

Today in the Church we acknowledge the presence of the Holy Spirit *in* the believer. Yes, God lives in us! We emphasize the work of the Holy Spirit *upon* the believer and in the midst of the congregation. Yes, God's anointing is vitally important! But we have largely ignored the work of the Holy Spirit *through* the believer.

God wants to bless others *through* us, just like He did with His Son. He wants to pour out freely from His place of residence inside of us. Jesus said, *He that believeth on me, as the scripture hath said, out of his belly shall flow rivers of living water* (John 7:38, KJV). The "rivers of living water" don't flow *around* us; they flow out *through* us—*through* the core of who we are.

To me, this gives new meaning to the verse: ***Work out** your own salvation with fear and trembling; for it is God who works in you both to will and to do* *for His good pleasure* (Philippians 2:12-13). Truly salvation is in us—in our spirits. But God's desire is that we work it out—through our souls—so that it becomes visible to the world.

This is the era of "inside-out" glory. God intends for His life and love inside of us to radiate from the spirit, to the soul and out through the body. We were designed to be clothed with His glory, not as it comes down from above, but as it comes up from within. It is *Christ **in** you, the hope of glory* (Colossians 1:27). Much like a beam of light shines from a lighthouse, so the glory of God is meant to shine out of our bodies.

When Jesus died on the cross, He bowed His head and said, *It is finished!* (John 19:30). On the cross He paid the full price. He was both wounded and bruised. *He was wounded for our transgressions, He was bruised for our iniquities* (Isaiah 53:5). A wound bleeds outward; His wounds covered our manifest sin—transgressions that come out through the body. A bruise bleeds inward; His bruises covered silent, internal iniquities of the heart. He accomplished everything of restoration for us. His work is finished!

The only thing we have to do is believe.

I thank God for pressing me into that belief. What mystery in our loving Father who withholds the blessings we want in order to stir up in us a desire for richer blessings that He then showers upon us. Until trials and sufferings cracked the façade of my "good Christian" life, I felt no need to know God in a deeper way. It was these sin afflictions that pushed me deep, deep down into the love of God . . . so I could learn of His ways . . . and be part of His cure.

It is wonderful to know that God does not want to "get rid of me," "work around me" or just "come down to bless me." The essence of my character and personality—my soul—is precious to Him. When He formed me in Mama's womb, He created my unique personality. He wants to give me more and more of Himself, so I can be more and more myself, so creation can become more and more itself—as He designed it to be.

Our God-created destiny is on the horizon.

Our souls long for it.

CHAPTER 23

Soul Cry

Several years ago, I remember standing in the driveway at the house in San Luis Obispo where I grew up. It was just after Christmas 2005, early on in this love/soul journey, and my Camry was loaded down with the kids' suitcases ready for the six-hour drive home. The apple trees in the orchard had lost their leaves, and the hills I had explored as a youth with Sunshine and Degan were not yet splashed with even a hint of green.

A light rain fell, but the wind whipping my hair told of greater storms to come before the spring. Daddy walked down the stone steps from the house and put his hand on my shoulder. I looked up into his face framed with his graying hair, damp but not soaked enough to lose its curl.

"Mary, dear," he said, "remember, these momentary light afflictions are working in you an eternal weight of glory" (see 2 Corinthians 4:17).

During the turbulent years that have followed, that image of Daddy standing there in the early stages of the storm has stayed etched in my mind and served as the backdrop to God's promises.

Once, when a dear friend asked how to pray for me and my family, my response surprised even me. "Don't pray against the momentary light afflictions," I told her. "Pray for the eternal weight of glory."

The afflictions, however, have seemed anything but momentary and light. It hurts to have my dreams shattered so that the desires of my heart come to reflect His highest and best. Many nights I have fallen asleep on a pillow wet with tears. "Dennis, I'm lonely. We need you." On some days, sadness and powerlessness have threatened to overwhelm me. "Oh Jake, what can I do? Please. Please. Be okay."

In the course of these trials, a longing to have something I couldn't put into words—something beyond my conscious comprehension—grew in me. I struggled to understand, but I did not know what I was seeking to gain understanding of . . . or if it really even existed.

Some days it felt like I was trying to put a 2,000-piece jigsaw puzzle together without having the picture on the box top to guide me. Hundreds of Scriptures floated in my mind. Each one had to fit for the picture to be whole. They had to be tied together, all key parts of the same great plan. But how did they mesh? Where was I to begin? What did the big picture look like? And how was this to be the answer to the problems confronting my family and my lack of love?

I prayed for answers . . . and for right questions. I lay on the floor in the living room quiet before God. I shared my thoughts and listened to others share theirs. I studied the Bible like I had never studied it before. Some days I walked for miles, not really paying much attention to where I was going—just meditating, processing, listening to God. When I felt I needed confirmation about what God was showing me, a book, sermon or verse would "just happen" to come to my attention.

In all of this, I remembered what Jill had said that day in Sunday school: "If it's God, it has to be simple." I knew that was true. But I had to reconcile simplicity with hundreds of Scriptures that didn't fit into any sort of big-picture framework of understanding for me. It had to be simple alright—uncomplicated enough for a child to grasp—but it also had to be complete.

And slowly, bits of the whole, beautiful puzzle came together. First I began to understand about the fig leaves, then about the spirit, soul and body, and then about the two trees and our God-created purpose from the beginning. And each piece fit together with the others in love.

Incredible! The life He designed us for is INCREDIBLE!

Jesus said, *Most assuredly, I say to you, he who believes in Me, the works that I do he will do also; and greater works than these he will do, because I go to My Father* (John 14:12). Jesus made a way for us to do the works of God just as He did!

Second Peter 1:3-4 tells us, *His divine power has given to us all things that pertain to life and godliness, through the knowledge of Him who called us by glory and virtue, by which have been given to us exceedingly great and precious promises, that through these you may be partakers of the divine nature.* We were created to be "partakers of the divine nature"—Christlike in the core of our being!

However, what we experience in this world and what we read in God's Word are not in agreement. The truth of these "exceedingly great and precious promises" is vastly discrepant from our experience of reality. A chasm of difference separates the Holy Scriptures from our life in this world . . . to date.

But life experience will come to match the fullness of the truth as we hold onto that truth by faith. When we take the Word and renew our minds with it, that truth will be proved out as the will of God! Scripture tells us, *And do not be conformed to this world, but be transformed by the renewing of your mind, that you may prove what is that good and acceptable and perfect will of God* (Romans 12:2).

And so I cling to His Word, give Him my heart and then cry for Him to bring forth what my heart really wants. I can't pretend that life is okay with war and bloodshed, cancer and mental illness, drug abuse and divorce. God didn't create the earth to be in this state, and He didn't create us human beings to take it all in stoic silence.

These days I'm choosing to see my world as it really exists—full of messed-up people burdened down with sin because of Satan's life-destroying lies. And I'm choosing to see what Scripture really says—about how we are to be part of the cure. And I'm aligning myself with God's Word . . . until my soul's desire becomes reality and life is made right in the love of God.

It will be!

At this time in history, a massive paradigm shift is starting to take place. Two streams are flowing. Both are gaining strength as they move in the same direction—toward wholeness in Christ. One is the stream of love, and the other is the stream of healing for the soul.

More and more these days, I am hearing about love from preachers, evangelists and missionaries around the world. From the slums of Mumbai to the auditoriums of Harvard University, love is being proclaimed. People, from little-known authors to famous speakers, from conservative Baptists to radical Pentecostals, are starting to understand and live out different pieces of the beautiful mosaic of His all-encompassing love.

But we have to get it right and know that the love God designed to flow out of us comes only from Him. If we don't realize this, we'll be fooling ourselves like I was until that day at Edna's when this whole journey began.

The stream of soul healing is gaining momentum too. Agnes Sanford first brought understanding about soul care to the Church. In the 1940s, 50s and 60s, her pioneering work came to be called by others, "healing of the memories." John and Paula Sandford took up her work and pressed on through the 1980s.

Today the process of soul healing takes many forms, some of which may be referred to as "theophostic counseling," "SOZO" or "inner healing." The names we give Jesus' work of healing our mind, will and emotions are not important. The critical thing is that we are learning that Jesus came to heal the brokenhearted and set the captives free. The Church at large is starting to understand the importance of soul healing in making us whole and freeing our minds to embrace God's glorious intent for us.

When these two streams—love and soul healing—merge, the river will be unstoppable. When we're around people who love us like Jesus does, we'll start believing that God really does love us. And believing He loves us will help us open ourselves up to Him so He can purify the soul . . . and pour in more love . . . and purify still further . . . and pour in yet more love.

That one free-flowing river will change the face of Christianity forever . . . because it is in our souls that the love of heaven becomes the love the world so desperately needs.

The will of God touches earth in our souls! We are meant to be the answer to Jesus' prayer: *Thy kingdom come. Thy will be done in earth, as it is in heaven* (Matthew 6:10, KJV). God intends that His will be done on earth by having expression in us! His light, life and love come to earth in physical reality in us!

Everything in God's will is based upon His love. Everything in the kingdom is love motivated, love energized and love producing. Every aspect of His will for us has as its foundation the one New Commandment: *A new commandment I give to you, that you love one another; as I have loved you, that you also love one another* (John 13:34).

In the kingdom of God, everything we receive is love based and everything we give is love generated. We are a part of the kingdom. Scripture tells us, *The kingdom of God is* ***within you*** (Luke 17:21, KJV). Nothing can be in the kingdom except what follows the law of the King, and His law is love.

And His kingdom will be a growing, expanding one. *We are more than conquerors through Him who loved us* (Romans 8:37). We are soldiers meant for the awesome task of expanding His kingdom of love on earth. We become conquerors by sharing the love He pours into us with the world.

When I had cried out in the Mumbai airport, "Isn't God's love supposed to conquer all this?" I'd not understood. But now I see. God's love *through* us will conquer.

Deep within us is a longing to be conquerors and see things set right in the love of God. Rightness is stamped solidly into the core of our original formation. My soul desires that His love be made lavishly known to me and to my world. I want to be filled with the *zoe* life and love of God. "Life! Love! Freedom!" is my cry.

Indeed all of creation groans for the "glorious liberty" God's children will share with it. *For the earnest expectation of the creation eagerly waits for the revealing of the sons of God. . . . The creation itself also will be delivered from the bondage of corruption into the glorious liberty of the children of God* (Romans 8:19, 21).

My soul leaps in joyful anticipation. A whole new way—the way of God's plan from the beginning—is on the horizon!

I'm starting to see it in my own life. I'm stepping into the joy and freedom of life in the love of God. And it's rubbing off on others too.

CHAPTER 24

"Mary, Thank You for Loving Me."

The freshly painted, even-brighter yellow on Edna's mobile home greeted me from afar when I went for a visit the other day. Edna met me at the door like she always did—with a hug and a smile. "Mary, it's so good to see you."

We sat back in our identical stuffed rocking chairs to enjoy the pleasant May afternoon. Edna's ivory-colored, satin pajamas complemented the chair fabric perfectly; I couldn't help thinking that she fit that chair like a matched pillow.

In between sips of green tea, we read from the first part of Hebrews. When we came to the part about entering the rest, Edna stopped me. She told me a story about picking flowers on the way home from school when she was in second grade and falling asleep in the field.

She had grown up the ninth of 10 children in rural Oklahoma. Her dad had left the family when she was 6, but she remembered him bouncing her on his knee.

She talked. I listened. She talked some more. Most of the stories I'd heard before. But just like a child who requests the same bedtime story over and over again, I enjoyed the retelling.

When it came time to leave, Edna put her hands on my shoulders. Her intense blue eyes looked straight into mine.

"Mary, thank you for loving me," she said.

People are saying things like that to me more and more these days. As my soul becomes whole, I am finding that rather than doing things to earn love, I am doing things just because I love. Life seems easier. The freedom I had experienced as a teenager, roaming the hills with Degan, Sunshine and my Bible, is something I am coming to live in every day in this world of people and problems.

Some days the song I had listened to over and over again on that second trip to India comes singing back to me. *I have been blind, unwilling, to see the true love you're giving. . . . And I feel my heart is turning, falling into place.* I am seeing the love He has for us, and deep inside of me, things are falling into place. My soul is coming home to rest in the love of God.

The longing of my soul as I threw rose petals along the narrow country road in front of our farmhouse is being fulfilled. Jesus is touching me with His love, but not in the way I thought it might happen when I had prayed in the alfalfa field evening after evening. The love of heaven is flooding my soul. I'm allowing Him kingship there. The rubber is meeting the road—in the soul.

His love is flowing out of me to others and the world. I'm coming to relate to others soul-to-soul with God's love.

And that same love is coming back to me through them. I'm learning of God's love by receiving theirs.

That is changing me. . . . That is changing us. Together we are casting off the lies, believing in His love and getting free to love others and to be loved by them. We are seeing God's life and love through each other.

One day not too long ago, a lightness in the room greeted me when I walked into the morning prayer meeting. My friends were moving around, praying in happy voices. Jill was dancing to music I couldn't hear.

Carl started singing, and we all—Pastor Andy, Jill, Floyd and the rest who were there—joined in.

I've got a river of life flowing out of me
Makes the lame to walk and the blind to see
Opens prison doors, sets the captives free
I've got a river of life flowing out of me.

Spring up oh well within my ***soul***
Spring up oh well and make me whole
Spring up oh well and give to me,
That life abundantly.

How many times before had I sung that song? But now those familiar words blossomed with new understanding and caught me up in joyful anticipation. What a battle! What a victory!

Now may the God of peace Himself sanctify you entirely; and may your spirit and soul and body be preserved complete, without blame at the coming of our Lord Jesus Christ.

Faithful is He who calls you, and He also will bring it to pass (1 Thessalonians 5:23-24, NASB).

Amen and Amen.

AFTERWORD

I have been taught that books are supposed to end with the problems and questions presented in the first chapters resolved in the end.

This book fits that model . . . but not in the way I had hoped when the story first began. The things I'd prayed for in the Mumbai airport didn't get resolved in the way I wanted. Jake didn't don a cap and gown and participate in the commencement exercises at Harvard. Dennis didn't get down on one knee with a bouquet of red roses and a re-engagement ring.

No. This book ends with something bigger than my original perspective on how a good story should conclude. Deep inside of me, questions and problems are being laid to rest in an unfolding cure too glorious for me to fully comprehend.

One day just after finishing an earlier draft of this book, I was feeling pretty cocky. It had been an incredible journey. I now understood how God had created us to be fully alive with His love flowing through spirit, soul and body. We Christians are meant to be watercourses carrying His light, life and love to a hurting world. In this way, God's love is delivered to others in a language they can understand so that they too can embrace the Source of that love. He made us humans to share His heavenly love with the world... But He stopped me short in my elevated musings.

In a sense, this book is like a blueprint. It details on paper the way God created us to function.

But a blueprint of a building isn't the building itself; a blueprint of a bridge does nothing to actually get one across the raging torrents. God gave Noah specifications for building the ark, but it wasn't the plan that saved him, his family and the animals; it was the actual boat.

And so it is with this book; it's just a blueprint—of the Master's plan.

But blueprints are a starting point . . . for the completed work. You and I are meant to be that work—the masterpiece of His design.

Eagerly I await!!!

SELECTED BIBLIOGRAPHY

Buckingham, Jamie. *Daughter of Destiny: Kathryn Kuhlman . . . Her Story.* New Jersey: Logos International, 1976.

Dew, Bill, and Carol Dew. *Living Free—Sozo Training.* Dewnamis Ministries, 2003.

Eldredge, John. *The Journey of Desire.* Nashville: Thomas Nelson Publishers, 2000.

Enns, Gaylord. *Love Revolution: Rediscovering the Lost Command of Jesus.* Xulon Press, 2009.

Groban, Josh. "My Confession." *Closer.* CD released 11/11/2003.

Joyner, Rick. *There Were Two Trees in the Garden.* New Kensington, PA: Whitaker House, 1993.

Moseley, J. Rufus. *Perfect Everything.* Saint Paul, MN: Macalester Park Publishing, 1988.

Murray, Andrew. *Covenants and Blessings.* New Kensington, PA: Whitaker House, 1984.

Nee, Watchman. *The Spiritual Man.* New York: Christian Fellowship Publishers, Inc., 1977.

Sanford, John A. *The Kingdom Within: A Study of the Inner Meaning of Jesus' Sayings.* New York: J.P. Lippincott Company, 1970.

Sandford, John, and Paula Sandford. *The Transformation of the Inner Man.* New Jersey: Bridge Publishing, Inc., 1982.

Willard, Dallas. *Renovations of the Heart.* Colorado Springs, CO: Navpress, 2002.

Zodhiates, Spiros. *The Complete Word Study New Testament.* Chattanooga, TN: AMG Publishers, 1992.

CONTACT INFORMATION

FOR SPEAKING REQUESTS

maryandfriendsbook@yahoo.com

530-757-2749

TO ORDER MORE BOOKS

Uncovering Love, Discovering Soul
by Mary and friends

or

Love Revolution:
Rediscovering the Lost Command of Jesus
by Gaylord Enns

www.LoveRevolutionPress.com

info@LoveRevolutionPress.com

530-891-5599